To the Moon and Back

A journey of the soul...

by Liz Roy

Little Mountain Publishing
Vancouver Island, B.C.

Library and Archives Canada Cataloguing in Publication

Roy, Liz, 1951-
To the moon and back :
a journey of the soul-- / Liz Roy.

Includes index.
ISBN 978-0-9781109-3-2

1. Roy, Liz, 1951- Travel--South America.
2. South America--Description and travel.
3. Mind and body. I. Title.

F2225.R69 2008 918.04'4 C2008-901348-4

Little Mountain Publishing
Parksville, B.C. Canada
email: inquiries@little-mountain-publishing.ca
website: www.little-mountain-publishing.ca

This book is dedicated to

Robert & Mark Broerse,

Gil Roy

& Josie, my mother

TABLE OF CONTENTS

Table of Contents *cont'd*

The real voyage of discovery consists not in seeking new landscapes but in having new eyes.

~Marcel Proust

TO THE MOON AND BACK

A Journey of the Soul ...

I want to tell you how I arrived at the title of this book.

My two sons and I were sitting in the café at a Barnes and Noble Book Store in Bellingham, Washington, where they 'proudly served' Starbucks coffee. At the next table was a tow-headed little boy about six or seven years of age. Sitting beside his mother, he blurted out, "I love you to the moon and back!" This admission thrilled our conversation to a halt. We smiled at each other then over at the boy.

Being a mother, I knew the import of these words and hoped the mother did, as well. To be so full of love, so full of life and then be able to express it so succinctly is a God-given gift. I carried this scene, those words, through the years and hoping the time was right, decided to use it as my title.

My memoirs carry with them great significance because they include those from past lives – in essence, time travel. The rest includes 'this life' travels to South America, travel back to my past plus many oblique and not so oblique observations of people and certain incidents, which also certainly helped to shape the ME that is me.

We may not go 'to the moon and back' but it will be a great trip, nonetheless.

A DEAD RACCOON

As I was travelling on the Island Highway near my home in Parksville, I happened to notice a strange scene on the side of the road. There was an old pickup truck and then a few yards behind was a dead raccoon propped against the concrete abutment.

A yard or so away was the driver of the truck squatted down, gazing upon the poor animal, his chin upon his hand. It almost looked as if he were carrying on a conversation with the creature casually leaning like a friend who has all day to answer with comments and questions. Were the man and the raccoon talking about philosophy or psychology as in the state of the universe and/or the elitism of the common mind? Were they gossiping about a mutual acquaintance, trading recipes or bemoaning the lack of good, arable land? A smile teased my lips as I drove on.

The real truth is the sadness of the scene and my heart went out to the man who must have kneeled as a sad requiem to the life he had accidentally extinguished under the wheels of his truck. He perhaps took a moment to send an apology to the spirit of the animal. I like to hope that's what he was doing.

This image has stayed with me for over a year, which gives rise to two questions. Why did this scene stay with me and why did the driver stop? After all, many people would have driven on and considered the death of a creature an inconvenience, mere messy roadkill beneath the tires.

The fact that the trucker did not carry on after hitting the creature but stopped to survey and study it with wonder and regret is the first answer. As to the second question, it could be he was announcing some form of spiritual connection to the beast just as an aboriginal kills a creature with his arrow and then takes the time to bless it and send its spirit to its heavenly home.

It's the connection, that golden umbilicus that binds us to our corporeal bodies and binds us, man to beast and man to man. A bond that sadly many of us do not feel, let alone see. But it is there, all the same, an energetic, synergistic force that turns the world and influences the stars in the firmament and the galaxies beyond. We all have within us that force and power, to metaphorically move mountains or bring a lover back to our side with our longing, (which is another form of energy, not as positive but just as potent.)

By sharing my recollections, I want to forge an invisible bond between my readers and me. Many of these memories are sad, a little tragic but they helped form and strengthen my spirit. They comprised a four-month trek to South America (ending in Mexico City), memories of my youth and memories of past lives. While I travel, you travel with me. What I feel, you feel. When I hurt, we hurt together. Then we heal together.

As for the dead raccoon, I am just beginning to realize that the power that fuels the great things in our lives also fuels the not-so-great things, like corporate greed. However, I don't think I would have observed someone with a suit and briefcase on the side of the highway kneeling bewitched in front of a dead raccoon.

Yet in the times to come, that just may happen.

EYES OF A CHILD

I wave my hands in the air, not only to comfort myself but also to amaze myself with the extraordinary newness of my body. My eyes are sometimes slightly blurry but usually I can focus on the changing faces hovering over my bassinet. Mostly I look for my mother's face.

She studies me, not as a mother enamored by her newly-born child but as a scientist whose clinical eye studies a monkey or guinea pig in a cage. Or like a child who curiously observes an insect bobbling around inside a grassy jar.

She doesn't hate me, though she didn't want me. All the forces inside her have bottled the resentment, the unhappiness of the arrival of her fifth (and thankfully last) fleshly burden.

I am so innocent but my soul, so old and wise. I, too, have battled with this heartache, even as I listlessly tarried beneath her beating heart. Inside her worn-down womb, I knew my arrival would never know an exhausted, joyous shout of welcome. Would never know the tender parting of my swaddling blanket to explore my fingers, my toes and parts of my face, to assure her I was complete and normal.

Whether I was normal or not, didn't matter to my mother. She was already exhausted and beaten down before my father expended his seed within her womb. Insidiously, selfishly I grew when she least wanted or expected another. I could not blame her, I really couldn't, but wasn't I just an innocent, newborn child?

What did I know except the hunger bubbling in my tummy, or the cold, clammy wetness of the waste that expelled too often from the tiny apertures between my legs? I craved and expelled the sated craving with alarming regularity. In between, I slept and cried for the face, that special face, to appear above me.

She little knows how much I study her as she studies me. How tired and even scared she looks, with thin, wispy hair framing a worn, prematurely aged face. Her eyes are a pretty shade of green. If she had the inclination, a bit of color might have set them off nicely but there is neither time nor reason.

My father is the reason. Only a few times has his face hovered above me. Each time, my little body reacts by folding up in horror and screaming with the primal pain of fear. Yet his face isn't ugly, it is handsome. I see black eyes like mine, swarthy skin like a gypsy and a very thin moustache above thin lips. Like my mother, he studies me intently and curiously but there is a proud cruelty to his look and I know why.

He enjoyed the exhaustion of my mother, enjoyed that he had trapped her once again with his sperm into unwanted motherhood. She was not only the repository of his seed but also the vessel to receive the frustration of all of his dreams unfulfilled and my every cell and corpuscle knows it and holds it.

My aunt, my mother's sister, has come to help my mother with me and my other three sisters and one brother. Her touch is gentle and she seems to enjoy holding me, feeding me and doesn't even mind waking in the night to change my soiled diapers. I want my mother so bad, want her to want me as much as I need her, but she, my aunt, will have to do.

She carries the same expressions as my mother but her face is not riddled with strain and futility. I hear her sing as she folds the cotton nappies beside my crib. When I gurgle she bends over me and chucks my cheek. I hope she stays with us for a long time. Yet deep inside, I know she will go and cold reality will have to be faced and survived.

Why, why did I choose this god-forsaken family to be born into? Before I was flesh, I was spirit-in-waiting. Was there a shortage of loving parents down below, who dreamed together of a precious firstborn? Could I have waited longer for the next batch of good ones? Or was there just so much time in which to wait and if I didn't put my spirit down, then I'd miss my chance? Knowing this loveless circle for such a time as I've been here in flesh, I should have stayed where I was. Even if it took a millennia or two to find the perfect life, I should have bided my time. I must have been impatient or not checked the roster of incarnations as carefully as I should have. Everything here so far looks dismal for me. Once my aunt leaves, I fear it may take longer before my mother will answer my cries for milk and care.

In the hospital, she could barely feed me, her breasts were so small and dry. The nurses tut-tutted over her, cheered her on and thankfully she produced for their sake, not for mine.

I am so hungry here at home. She does try to satisfy me but it is never enough and I don't mean to cry but I cannot help myself. My poor mother, my poor me. I have wished many times she would just take me into her arms and cry with me, if she needed. But she does not cry; there are no tears left in her. She does not know that when I cry, I cry for both us. Not only for what is now, but for the long, lonely road ahead.

What will be? I can already see a dull, gray slab of an early life with a few straggling, struggling flowers growing between. A shy, frightened child hiding behind the thing or person she needs to hide most from. A defiant, sarcastic teenager, who challenges and mocks authority, to her own learning detriment. A bitchy girlfriend, a compliant wife. And why compliant, after all the fighting and scrapping?

Because, like her mother, she knows it to be an expedient ruse, but an exhausting one at that. And what is left is what her husband will get.

That is still to come but surely pre-ordained. I am still here in my bassinet, waving my hands in the air, mesmerized by how such tiny miracles of nature can capture and hold the light.

GO TO YOUR OWN CORNER

Seven months after returning from South America, I asked my partner to leave.

I'll give you a clear picture of what lead up to this. We had moved out of our huge house in Nanaimo on Vancouver Island in April of 2006, to our motor-home, then parked it in the trailer park we owned south of the city. Then, a few weeks later, we moved into a tiny trailer at an RV Resort in Parksville. We bought a lot in the resort, bought a new trailer to put on it and moved into that during the latter part of June. We lived in it for several months, then flew to Peru and Ecuador at the end of November. Travelling by bus, we lived in hostel rooms, many of them very tiny (sometimes the hostels were very 'hostile'). At the end of February, we flew to Mexico City and stayed there for over a week before returning home to our two-roomed trailer at the beginning of March 2007. It was the rainiest summer ever and often we spent days confined to our small space at the resort. We accepted an offer for the sale of our mobile home park but the deal fell through. We had hoped to buy a 'real' home, where we could find our own space to stretch and spread out. But it was not to be.

I live or lived with a retired lawyer and do you know what that is like? I will share a snippet of conversation:

He: Did you like that dish? Did you think it was too spicy?

Me: Well..a little.

He: What do mean? Either it's spicy or it's not.

Me: Well…

He: Answer yes or no.

Me (stubbornly): No, I am not going to answer the way you want me to.

He: You're being evasive. When people are being evasive, they're not telling the truth.

Me: I am NOT being evasive. I'm just thinking about your question.

He: It's a logical question and I don't know why you can't give me a simple answer.

Me (philosophically): Well, life is not that simple or logical.

He: Now, you're really being evasive. What are you trying to hide?

Me (thinking): I am trying to hide my urge to smack you one.

Me: Weren't we talking about spice? Am I on the witness stand here?

He: All I asked was a simple question about how spicy this dish is. Why is it so difficult for you to give me a straight answer?

Me: Because you want one.

He: And what is that supposed to mean?

And so on….

Now you can see I have the capability to bait my partner because I don't like being trapped like a cat in a cage. In many hours of counseling, we have learned that he is an 'auditory-digital' person, one who thinks in sequence, like a digital clock and through reasoning, arrives at a logical result. As for me, I am 'kinesthetic' as I regard life as more or less a philosophical, experiential exercise. There is no end result because life is one long, rambling discussion and I usually express myself with, "I feel…" When I walk into a room full of strangers, I allow my gut to assess the energy of the people there. My partner walks in and commands the room.

When two polar opposites occupy a small space and both are strong, intelligent personalities, it is a powder keg waiting to explode. And it exploded Thanksgiving weekend – over a bag of apples.

Why was that my tipping point? Why couldn't it be something monumental like an infidelity or a slap in the face? No, that never happened – ever.

He had brought, from our trailer park, a big bag of apples and I 'felt' he expected me to peel, core and produce applesauce. Somehow that perceived expectation enraged me. Dragging the bag of apples to the counter, I proceeded to annihilate them. To my partner's credit he had been suffering a sinus infection but I felt he overplayed it at times.

Nasty words were exchanged and the result was I asked him to leave. Within days he had moved into another trailer across the resort.

It's only been a week but a week fraught with sleepless nights and second-guessing.

However, the advantages of this new state of affairs are boundless. Because I need a great deal of peace and quiet, I now have it. I can now write this book that has been brewing inside of me ever since we returned from South America. He can now spread his stuff everywhere without my incessant complaining. I can read a book and listen to opera to my heart's content. He can play all the music he has downloaded on his computer without using a headphone. (He hates opera.) I can make a meal whenever I feel like it and add those ingredients he regarded as too expensive or not to his taste. He can now eat all the chile and beans his little stomach desires. I can leave the sponge on the sink. (He hates that.) He can leave the dishes *in* the sink. (I hate that.) He can, I can…

Without saying, we've decided to approach our 'new' relationship from a friendship point of view, with a bit of courtship thrown in. Respect and appreciation. Hopefully.

We never knew courtship, my partner and me. We courted by long distance phone calls and then a summer visit. I returned home to sell and pack my belongings. Then back in his home, in a domestic arrangement. Practical for him, perhaps, but unromantic for me. My heart ached to know the wait for his arrival to escort me to the symphony or to a play. To dress up and enjoy long, lingering dinners on an ocean quay. To wonder where he was when I wasn't with him. All I wanted was to feel his protective arm around my waist, to wonder if this would be the night we'd spend together in lovemaking, him pulling me to spoon inside his crescent body to feign sleep. Instead, it was me being the wife, fulfilling domestic duties while he, the important lawyer, went off to his office. Me, I awaited his tread on the stair in order to microzap his dinner.

Now, here is our chance to actually provide the missing ingredient. I invited him for lunch today. Will he try to make out with me?

AT THE TOP OF THE STAIRS

Many times over the years, my father told me the story about how my mother threatened to toss me down the stairs when I was just a baby.

She must have been very depressed and very distraught to even consider this. But to my father, that didn't matter. What mattered was, her behavior elevated him to a higher moral level because, as he said, "What kind of mother would do a thing like that? Toss a baby down the stairs or threaten to do it?" The threatening was as sinful as the act.

While my father recounted this tale, his eyes burned with cruel, wicked glee. Usually, I listened silently and stolidly, never asking questions but always wanting him to finish, to get it over with, like downing a dose of bad medicine. I always wondered, though, what purpose did it serve telling me this horrific tale? One answer was to demonstrate how little my mother wanted me. Another answer was to show how far her mental state had deteriorated. To me, the man who stood at the bottom of the stairs was the real cause.

Now, so many years later, I wished I had asked the questions. Even now, I wonder if both my parents lied. Was I sent tumbling down the wooden steps, bumpety bump bump? If so or not, the damage, not to my body, lingers still – here in my soul.

Can you imagine that innocent child? How ignorant was she of the danger she faced? Her mother must have stood at the top of the stairway holding her and rocking her. Not to comfort, but because she was in such a state of agitation and perhaps even anger.

I only assumed my father stood at the bottom of the stairs, yet do not know if he arrived at the almost-last moment to talk my mother out of her craziness. Or whether they had been arguing back and forth and, as the arguing escalated, grew more heated, she began to threaten my life.

My father wished me to show anger towards my mother for what she almost-did. But I couldn't. I sensed what he was trying to do. I refused to get caught up in his need to punish my mother, to chastize her lack of nurturing, her lack of responsibility. To exchange his need for the loss of my sense of security. He needn't have worried. I never knew a sense of security; he'd won, by punishing both my mother and me.

The more he dragged out this weary tale, the more I resented him, but I never asked him why. I just assumed my father was not intelligent or self-aware enough to know why. I merely assumed what I assumed; that above his judgment of my mother and even above his moral superiority, my dad felt he had rescued me. I should be forever grateful for his altruistic intervention.

My parents divorced when I was about eleven or twelve and this certainly was a long time coming. The only reason my mother had the courage was because my two older sisters talked her into it. She possessed no inner fortitude of her own and perhaps she would have stayed with him until the very bitter end. The ironic thing was, her threatening the life and limb of her youngest child was perhaps one of the few forays into a display of gumption she may have ever known with this man. Something to think about, anyway.

LIMA, PERU

Sitting in a large square in the great city of Lima, we believed it to be the site of an art institute and museum. We were too tired to avail ourselves of this particular Liman culture, as two days of travel had worn us down to a comatose nub. We found a park bench, partially shaded, where we listened to the cooing of doves, the cooing of young lovers and the distant cacophony of taxis and minibuses beyond the imposing gates. We were forced to walk the streets as we checked out of our hotel at one o'clock and our flight to Trujillo didn't depart until 8:30 in the evening. How could we occupy ourselves for about four hours when all we wished to do was find a soft bed and sleep the afternoon away?

We had taken two days to get to Lima. We'd left Vancouver Island on the 20th of November, stayed with friends on the mainland, then flew to Toronto on the 21st. The weather was cold and an icy chill kept us in our hotel room most of the day. We took a shuttle to the airport early to make certain we would not miss this very important flight.

I felt as if I had no ground beneath my feet, even felt as if my feet belonged to someone else. What awaited us there, in such a faraway country? Fears of safety, fear of never returning to home, friends and family, I kept locked in the attic of my mind. I wanted to appear brave to Gil, ready to take on whatever he wanted to take on. If I pretended I was up to meeting the challenge, then the pretense would morph into reality. *I think intrepid, therefore I am.*

We had a great seat on the plane directly behind the bulkhead between business and coach class. Therefore there was a great deal of leg room for Gil, who usually opted for an aisle seat so he could get up, stretch his legs, walk around and generally be a nuisance to the airline personnel. However, there was an Oriental couple who had been split up, the husband sitting in the row behind his wife and baby daughter. She sat beside me and I realized I couldn't sit there, knowing a family was forced apart for such a long, long flight. I beckoned to the man and switched seats with him, sitting directly behind Gil so I could be a nuisance to *him*...

The child was a dream throughout the whole flight. She cooed, smiled, and slept while everyone around cooed and smiled back at her. A cot was set up directly in front of the mother and when she wasn't in her parents' arms, the little girl calmly laid on her back, gazing around contentedly or sleeping the sleep of the innocent. We learned that the mother was originally from Peru though she was of Chinese extraction; they were meeting her family at the airport.

When we arrived in Lima, I went up and said my good-byes to the sweet and loving family. When I told them their daughter was a joy to have on our journey, her parents said, "We are so lucky to have her", and I replied, "No, she is blessed to have you." They thanked me again for giving up my seat, then Gil and I went to search out the driver who was to take us to the hostel we had booked online.

It was dark, too dark to see what Lima looked like at night. We were tired and I felt a little shell-shocked, tried to pretend that we were visiting Mexico, a place a lot closer to home. I needed to take in the idea of 'far, far away' in increments. Besides, I had Gil, who was fearless, adventurous and tireless so what was the problem? The taxi dropped us off on a quiet side street, at the *Hostal de las Artes,* we paid the driver with the Soles we had bought at the airport and checked in.

The hostel must have been a hundred years old, at least. The ceilings were very high, the lighting very dim and our room emanated a slightly musty smell though the staff were very warm and welcoming. However, that night we barely slept because the noise of hammering and the thump of feet on floorboards in the room above prevented very little repose. In the morning, we felt as if we were hit by one of those same hammers. Getting dressed, we went to a great nearby restaurant for our breakfast.

Where Gil and I breakfasted on our first, official Liman morning, only business people frequented the restaurant. The waiters and waitresses all dressed formally in black pants and white shirts. We enjoyed toast, eggs and fresh coffee and the bill for the two of us came to about 12 Soles or $4. USD, a real bargain. Our belly pouches were full to bursting with our well-worn, exchanged cash and our real bellies full of delicious food.

Liman time is the same as Eastern Time, i.e., three hours later than our Pacific Time. Back home we would have been nibbling on a homemade muffin and sipping ground coffee while checking email on our respective laptop computers in the small trailer at Surfside R.V. Resort where we live in Parksville. Surfside, oceanside.

We found Surfside on the Internet. It's a 5-star R.V. resort smack on the oceanfront. Before the closing date of the sale of our house in Nanaimo, we drove to the resort, week after week, hoping to find a place to live temporarily. Through a real estate agent we found a 30-foot Golden Falcon trailer owned by a man whose wife had recently died of cancer.

The carpet was dirty and worn but the cabinetry was nice and the living area gave onto a large sunroom. This was April and the winds from the ocean blew fierce and cold.

Our time spent in the Golden Falcon was depressing. Perhaps if the trailer were newer or larger, I wouldn't have felt so emotionally low. Perhaps the energy of the dying wife permeated the place. We were also exhausted from the move, the change and the upheaval of our lives. (Much of what we'd owned in the house was sold, donated or stored.)

The so-called bedroom did not have a slide-out and was cramped, very cramped. The bed was referred to as a 'short queen' and to accommodate Gil's legs, we pushed out the mattress from the top, and filled the gap with our pillows.

STREET in LIMA

We couldn't spend very much time in the sunroom since it was still cold, rainy and windy, which did not lessen my sense of melancholy. We arranged to have the carpet cleaned but within two weeks it seemed that the same dirt forced its way up from the bottom and re-established pride of place on the surface. Like the carpet, I felt stained and worn.

Gil had wanted to go to South America for a long time, but I was afraid and stalled him for many years, citing a plethora of excuses, but finally I agreed. We booked the trip after moving into the new trailer we purchased on our new lot at Surfside. We sold the first trailer and lot at the end of August and, in November, we were on our way.

Liman streets are very similar to most streets in many large, Latin American cities. Garbage piles abound while friendly dogs roam free and unleashed, leaving their fecal and urinary offerings on every street corner. We walked over to the *Plaza de las Armas* to gaze at the immense bronze fountain. Nearby was the *Palacio de Gobierno,* where we heard they changed the guard just before noon. Adjacent to the large cathedral was a statue of Francisco Pisarro on horseback. Rumor had it that the horse's rear end had, at one time, faced - no, not faced, more like 'butted' – onto the front of the church. Since this was considered an affront to ecumenical pride, the statue was summarily moved to a more, ahem, dignified position.

We walked for several hours, endured many curious glances, as there were so few *gringos* on the streets. At a stoplight we watched four young men perform acrobatic stunts while cars impatiently idled. Their energy was boundless; they tumbled and flipped to earn tips from the drivers. How long could they last and was it worth what they received? Did they have a choice? In our country we have a welfare system, employment insurance, a form of safety net when some of us 'fall' financially. Here, in places like these, there is no such thing. I kept thinking as we passed sidewalk beggars, "There but for the grace of living in Canada, go I."

From the park in Lima, we caught a taxi to the airport. The flight to Trujillo was about an hour and a half. From there, it was a ten-minute cab ride to Huanchaco on the west coast.

Our friends from B.C. were to have arranged a room in their hostel, but when we got there, all the lights were out. After a bit of scurrying about, the owner summoned our friends. Somehow a mix-up had occurred and we were wiped off the blackboard that showed the schedule of reservations. 'Kay' and 'Dan' finally found us another place, but when we got there no one was in evidence. Finally a man appeared out of the darkness and told Gil we were to stay farther down the street at a 4-story building.

We dragged our suitcases there but soon realized we were caught in a scam. The owners just wanted to snag the business from the new place. Dragging our luggage back to the second hostel, we parked our butts on the side of the road. Our friends produced a bag filled with limes, rum, juice and paper cups. We toasted our first night in Huanchaco, Peru. Here's to the big adventure. A half-hour later, they helped us move into our hostel and we settled in.

In the middle of the night someone banged on the door. Gil went to answer it and there stood a couple of weary travelers looking for a place to crash. Gil sent him to the third hostel and we could hear them banging down the door in the distance. Poetic justice.

REED SEAHORSE - TRUJILLO HOTEL

THE BOY BEHIND THE MAN

Gil's dad was, at times, a violent man and often treated his eldest son cruelly, so I am told. Along the way the young boy who grew into a young man decided he would never be governed by emotions. Emotions caused a person to ball his hand into a fist ready to smash it against someone's face or body, resulting in not only physical harm to the person but harm to the suffering soul with the balled fist. So the young man walled in his emotions and consciously decided to give his life over to one master – principle. That way he couldn't be hurt by someone else's negative emotions. As long as everyone followed the rules, how could they get hurt? Principle was written in stone, and God forgive those who trespassed against it.

I told Gil that his principles were admirable but they broke hearts. They truly are lonely bedfellows.

DOMESTICITY

I stood at my kitchen sink
Like at a threshold
Looking back
Looking forward
Looking within
What I saw there
Made me take hold
Of a self now dead
Waiting to be re-born
So many feelings
Rushing up
                    And out
So many years wasted
So many worth the pain
                    I put in
I watched as the water
Swirled and whooshed
Down the drain
But I stood there still
Looking out the window
                    And beyond
Felt the breeze
Felt the ripples of my life
                    Filling me
Emptying out
Joy and sorrow
One thread
Keeping me alive

Brushing the soap
From my work-worn hands
A tear fell
Upon the dishes
Waiting to be dried

INSIDE AND OUT

I saw my mother on the birthing table. My soul gazed upon her contorted, angry, ugly face. Her hair hung in mangled tresses as the sweat oozed from every pore on her head and face. Her eyes were almost glazed save for a pinpoint of hate directed down between her legs. The anger, her misdirected anger, readied itself for my unwelcome arrival. A pact would be formed between her and me, the repository of her frustration and helplessness. It would be a pact, not borne of love, but of shame and guilt.

I arrived kicking, red-faced and squalling. In fact, my whole body was mottled red as if my mother blew the scarlet bile of her hate into my body and puffed it like a hot-air balloon. I was as ugly as she imagined, and she wanted to push me away but the nurses cajoled her along and because she was a good, obedient girl-mother, she took the child and held it, just barely, to her dried breast.

I squalled and demanded my due, my sustenance, but it would be a little time before the milk let down and so the nurses whisked me away to cuddle me, feed me the hospital's artificial formula and wrap me warmly in my cot.

She laid on the bed exhausted, relieved to have a respite from the demanding newborn. The hate was gone, drawn out of her. She knew it was somewhere down the hall, in a cot, mewling in its sleep. But soon the thing would awaken, then the steps back down the hall and she would be forced to give in, let down her gown, let down her guard and let down her breasts.

She thought of her husband; that was where the hate should be - with him. She felt suffocated and entrapped by their marriage. She had been so young, so naïve and he took her, pretended to be kind and gentle, but he was not. Far from it. He needled her and tried to goad her to match her anger with his, but she couldn't because that would mean they were well matched. And so she tamped down her hatred, bent her head and acquiesced.

She thought their fourth was her last. Their third child was a son but he wanted another to feed his ego. But it was another girl. The name chosen was swiftly changed to suit the sex. She knew this one would be a good one, knew they'd be alike. She'd be no trouble and would soon learn to play along, to please and placate, just like she did.

But then she got pregnant again. She tried to avoid him around the house and at bedtime but he knew – he figured it out. And one night, he forced her and afterward she felt hurt, angry and so ashamed. He was the one who should have been ashamed but instead he was triumphant. And here was the result demanding her lifeblood. Another girl, but just like him, or so it seemed.

Every time the child gazed up at her, she thought she saw her hate, hiding inside. The child screamed, not with hunger or wetness, but with fear. The pact was breaking. She was planning to destroy the contract by spilling the full-grown seed of her hate, cause it to be bludgeoned against the cold, hard and shiny hospital floor.

How she hated the squalling and the way she looked like him with her deep, dark almond eyes and black-brown hair. Anyone else would have cooed to it with delight but she had nothing left inside to offer – no voice, no heart - because her soul was dead from her life.

It was a monster and monsters must be destroyed no matter how small. She thought of the gremlins in the fairy stories and surely this must be one of them.

It would only take a nudge, a tap, and it would go flying. But then, what if it survived? What if she was forced to tend an idiot with a damaged mind?

She looked down at the floor. The bed, like all hospital beds, sat high. There was a railing but that could easily be pulled down if she wanted to get out to rock the child in the chair beside the bed. Oh God! Where to go? What to do? Tears squeezed from the corners of her eyes and slid down her bitter cheeks. How was she going to survive with this bundle of hate, newly arrived from her angry body?

No matter what, she was trapped. The courage left her

as it had left her so many times. I can bear this burden; I have no choice.

Wrapping the red-faced creature up again, she closed her eyes and placed its face against her breast. The milk immediately let down and she was grateful for that. Maybe a small connection could be forged, maybe the child will become more like her if she learns to curb her angry, demanding ways. It may take time, but she'll get the hang of it.

The pact, not broken, was patched by an inkling of a smile on her chapped, dry lips.

The child suckled but the fear nestled deeper inside her belly. Like a snake it wound around her soul and gave it a squeeze. Just remember, it cautioned the child, I'm here and I'll always be here. So be wary. Pacts made can be broken. Maybe not now, but later when you least expect it.

And so the child grew.

HECTOR, HUANCHACO & TRUJILLO

Though Huanchaco is on the ocean, the surrounding area on the northwest coast of Peru closely resembles a lunar landscape. Grey, hardpan hills with barely a scrap of tree or bush scalds the eyes and causes them to cast back towards the sky and surf. Otherwise, it is a typical tourist town with a plethora of restaurants, hostels, Internet cafés and even boasts a pier jutting out onto the ocean with a presiding guard, who collects a fee of a few Soles for the privilege of a stroll along its illustrious length.

Huanchaco's claim to fame are the reed boats or *caballitos,* which have been used for centuries and centuries by the fishermen, who paddle out to fish beyond the breakers and then, like outriggers, surf the waves back to shore with their catch. For a mere 1.50 USD, you could pretend you were a big 'kahuna' and ride out your dream. However, we were two weary travelers, more concerned with the armchair pursuit of Internet surfing, so we passed on the real thing.

Kay and Dan introduced us to Hector, who ran the Internet Café on the *malecon.* For 3 Soles (or 35 cents) an hour, we were able to email family and friends to let them know we'd arrived safely, assuage their worries and give our impressions of our new digs.

Hector was a well-built, affable South American who was born in Colombia, but had spent the better part of his life in Queens, New York. His English was impeccable and he was a fountain of knowledge and information about his native country, his adopted country, as well as life in Huanchaco. He knew the best places to eat, places to avoid and if you needed a translator to make future travel arrangements by phone, he was the man.

Hector introduced us to his wife, Anna, and their feisty son, barely two. He was determined to bring his child back to the States so he could learn English at a young age and then prepare him to assist in running the various enterprises he owned in Huanchaco when he grew up.

Hector referred to his wife as "Mona" and when questioned, he explained that light-haired, light-skinned Colombians were referred to as '*monas*' if female and '*monos*' if male. "However," he chuckled, "Monos here in Peru are a type of monkey, so we can't get our references confused."

Gil pointed to a poster on the wall of the café, which portrayed a modern, bullet-nosed train racing through a verdant landscape. Hector said this was his native Colombia.

"My country is very beautiful. What you know of it you have only heard in the media, about drug lords and danger. That is mainly in the jungles to the East. But if you travel on the West side, it is very safe. My people are warm and welcoming. There are many ex-patriots and they will tell you for themselves how much they love living there.

"The so-called *banditos* have issues with the government, not with the people or *turistas*. Sometimes they will empty a bus, but explain to the passengers they have no problems with them personally. Then they escort them to another bus and torch the first to make their point. No one gets hurt."

Hector paints a picture of Colombia that is new to our ears and minds. Its beauty, the friendliness of the people and, pointing to a map, suggests places that might appeal to two curious, cautious, Canadian travellers in South America. We stored his information in our mental backpacks and went back to the hostel to meet up with our friends.

Our hostel in Huanchaco looked like a grotto – literally. Inside the walls and the sink area someone had cemented large, grey river rocks. The floor was carpeted in a flat burgundy, which showed the dust emanating from the open area just outside our door. It was actually closed for renovations but the landlord/owner agreed to rent it to us for 15 soles a night, the equivalent of $5. U.S. We had to purchase our own water from the *tienda* (store) around the corner.

Often we'd return from an evening with Kay and Dan, having had dinner and roaming the beach, to discover that the front entrance was bolted closed. We'd be forced to sit on the curb, just like on our first night and wait for our concierge's apologetic return. We later learned he was on 'night watch', spending all night biking around the neigborhood, on the lookout for any suspicious activity. You could hear the bird-like 'tweet' of the whistles of fellow watchmen as they conducted their rounds and signaled to each other all was well in the quiet dark of Huanchaco.

Our first breakfast here was fine except for the 'coffee issue'. They didn't have fresh-roasted coffee. As a matter of fact, they didn't even *have* coffee. The young waiter took some money from the till, ran across the street to a nearby store and came back with a few packets of Nescafe'

RUINS OF CHAN CHAN OUTSIDE TRUJILLO, PERU

instant coffee. We suspected this set a precedent for our time in Huanchaco and we were later proved right. We opted for tea after that.

During our week with Kay and Dan, we took a *collectivo* (a Volkswagen mini-bus) to the thriving city of Trujillo, about a ten-minute drive away – but on this mode of transportation, a heck of a lot longer. There is a driver and an assistant. It is the assistant's job to collect the Soles for the ride (2 for both of us) and then pack as many people as possible inside the bus until there was no space between and no air to breathe. (The air I am kidding about, but not the space.) There are little or no shocks on these vehicles, which are usually past their prime, so it's a hard, rollicking ride into the city.

The Peruvians stared at us in curiosity and we made sure our pasted, polite Canadian smiles were in place. Since we hadn't spoken our version of Spanish for a very long time, we felt too shy to attempt contact, so little conversation was shared except with our friends. Kay and Dan, however, had been in South America a few months before us and seemed comfortable and chatty with the locals. Give us time.

En route, we passed the ruins of Chan Chan, the largest mud-brick city in the world. The Chimu had built it, a people who ruled the north coast before the arrival of the Incas (AD 1000-1470). Kay and Dan had toured the archaeological site and since they took a lot of digital photos, we decided this was enough for us. To be honest, it didn't look very inviting from where we sat, very dusty and the mounds in various stages of excavation. My excuse for laziness.

In Trujillo, we passed the great *ovalo* (traffic circle). Kay and Dan pointed out that this is where all the main bus stations are located. The mini-bus dropped us off at a market square. Open-air kiosks sold anything from the smallest trinkets to lovely shawls, embroidered blouses, hats, shoes and other clothing. We had decided to save our shopping for another time and rushed through to explore the colonial city.

Tiny cars were parked sardine-like, end-to-end on the streets and I wondered how a parallel park was managed. Since most of the vehicles sported a vast array of dents, I theorized they parked 'by feel'.

On a suggestion from our friends, we kept our backpacks in front and I held on to my roomy, khaki travel purse holding our digital camera. The sidewalks were very narrow and often we were forced to jump off to allow the many locals to barrel through and pass us. I felt overwhelmed by the press of people, by a sense of 'culture shock' and even a sense of loneliness. Loneliness, because

I felt as if I was the only person who didn't want to be here, didn't want to even pretend I wanted to be here. I longed to go home. For my partner's sake, I determined to enjoy myself, learn something, even if it killed me.

CABALLITOS DE HUANCHACO

A lot of the colonial mansions were painted in pastel colors, giving them an almost 'ice-cream' look. There were flavors of mint, pale strawberry and vanilla. Very pleasing to look upon but don't attempt a taste… These were once owned by Spanish nobles, who were drawn to Trujillo for the gold, silver and sugar plantations. Its founder, Francisco Pisarro, named the city after his birthplace in Spain. As the conquering people, the Spanish enslaved the original inhabitants, used them and abused them to rape the land of its natural resources. Here, so many centuries later, is one of the starting places. Such a benign present, such a cruel past.

HUANCHACO BEACH

LIZ & GIL - CASA DE LA EMANCIPACION

Thankfully, the rest of the group also felt overwhelmed by the crowds, so we slipped into the quiet of the *Casa de la Emancipacion* for respite. It was built in the time of Pisarro (about 1610 AD) and restored in 1970 by the Banco Continental. Since there were so few locals and tourists, we basically had the run of the place – save for the armed guards. The furniture was very dark and, of course, very ancient but someone had lovingly restored a lot of pieces to their original sheen. We took photos of each other in front of a 16th century fountain (no water) then bravely headed back into the crowd to look for lunch.

We found a partial open-air Chinese restaurant where we enjoyed Chow Mein, Coke and *cervezas* (beer). By this time we were too tired to shop, as the cool morning had been overtaken by the unending glare of the Peruvian sun and the endless press of the crowds. We opted to head back to Huanchaco, where we knew the ocean breezes would gently welcome our return.

FORGIVENESS

Forgive the sinner. Why is that, I wondered. Why should I feel for the person who hurt me so badly and on top of it all, seemed totally oblivious to my pain?

After a few regressions, I understood. A contract is made and it takes two to make it, two to break it. In order to move into my future, I needed to forgive – not necessarily forget – the one I entered the contract with.

Look at this: a child who, at 3 years old, developed a horrible skin condition. Even the name is so ugly, unsightly – **psoriasis.** *It is easier to tell people 'an allergy' or 'excema', which is the same thing as an allergy. More palatable, less repulsive.*

The hypnotherapist led me back. My family sat in the kitchen teasing and needling me; I felt so helpless, so alone. I was brought back to that moment in time so I could see, not just how hurt the child was, but how angry. It was there, very palpable. Through that, my decision, a pact formed with my mother to make her suffer her tacit condoning of the teasing. So my unsightly skin disease was born. My anger blazing on my skin, as if to say, 'here it is, mother, for you to see, because you did not protect me, allowed the cruelty, by not doing anything, not saying anything.'

Looking back at my life, I realize there was so little emotional support in my family. Instead we learned to psychologically manipulate to gain control. It wasn't just me who lacked support; none of us knew how to support each other.

My sister, next in age to me, got pregnant at 19. My mother, with her boyfriend, moved to an apartment out of town near the unwed mother's home where my sister lived until she gave birth, then gave up her child. I saw this and wondered if she would have done this for me. The answer I get back is, I don't think so. Her relationship with my sister was different, as they shared very similar qualities of personality. Though this sister appeared tougher, more confident on the outside, she was sensitive and insecure like my mother and this was their bond. I, too, was sensitive and insecure on the inside but my overt expression was needy and grasping. I couldn't blame my mother her preference, but there was that pact, you see.

Previously, the therapist had regressed me back to my birth, to the rejection of my being, through my mother's misplaced anger for her marital entrapment. But then, at three years old, I heard my soul cry out, 'I'll get you for this! You will suffer because I suffer. I will break out in sores all over my body. Then you will have to pay attention to me, feel sorry for me. And what is written on my body will be the mark of your rejection.' A pact of suffering – two ways.

Now, a freeing of the pact. Forgiveness for the creation of the pact. Forgive my mother, forgive myself. Both of us, punishers and victims, taking turns.

I could never imagine how it must have been to be married to my father. From my firsthand experience, he was a cruel, bitter person, seldom kind and used others as his scapegoats. He endlessly reeled out the story, like a yo-yo, of being treated cruelly by his own father, being sent out to work for a farmer who also treated him cruelly. Returning to visit his dad in a snowstorm, he knocked on the door of his father's home. His father opened the door, took one look at him and slammed it in his face. Now, that is cruel!

Yet, I never believed my father's story. To me, you see, being on the wrong end of cruel treatment should teach compassion for others. Been there, done that, won't do it again. Won't do it to others, because it hurts both ways. How can it be easy inflicting emotional, mental and physical pain upon another person? My father must have been stupid not to learn the lessons of the past. Or perhaps he refused to learn. Such stubbornness did not bode well for our whole family. Over time we inflicted our own brand of pain upon each other and did not have any idea how to feel compassion, how to emotionally support each other. There were no signposts to direct us, no ideas, and no recipes for our wellness. So we carried on as he did.

Over time, I took the route of self-analysis. My skin condition somehow forced me to look inward, examine the scars chafing my soul. I read hundreds of books looking for reasons, looking for understanding. If I could understand myself, my soul, then I could understand my family and from that would naturally flow a new sense of self-worth.

The understanding or the belief that my family and I had been together many lifetimes was both appealing and repulsive. I mean, how self-punishing can I be to come back to this? A means of perpetuating the self-abasement? And yet, yet... it could help me understand 'me' more.

If I could turn my experience around and regard it more as a gift than ongoing, perpetual wound-infliction, then my birth could be perceived like a movie projected on a blank screen, allowing me to remove the pain, get it out of the way.

First, the movie and then suddenly, the emotions rose up from deep within my sub-conscious, overwhelming and drowning me with hurt, rejection. But once the wounds re-opened through the regression, it also allowed me to climb inside my mother and see her point of view. I saw how she suffered and through her suffering, I could forgive her and thus forgive myself. 'Forgive us our trespasses as we forgive those who trespass against us...' Or, whom we ***perceive,*** *as trespassing against us.*

Perception as truth.

The thing is, at the very moment I healed my soul of this experience, did my mother also feel the grace, as well? Even though we live in the same province, we have only a small relationship. My eldest sister, a nurse, lives near my mother's group home and tends to her, visits with her, worries over her. They share this osmotic relationship not even death could rend. Truly, I don't want it, don't want the responsibility. I had no intention of rushing to her side after my enlightenment and suddenly igniting something that never was nor ever could be. It is what it is.

I know from my experiences, from my plethora of reading material that healing can happen if you just 'send it out'.

Once, during a psychic reading, I was told my father was in attendance. The reader told me he was in 'a cold place' and she didn't want to deal with it but he was asking for my forgiveness from beyond the veil of death. I replied that I had forgiven him and she looked me in the eye and asked, 'Out loud?' No, I hadn't. I went home, sat on the sofa my small inheritance had purchased and forgave him, 'out loud.' I didn't know there was a difference between thinking and speaking forgiveness. I guess there must be. Maybe it depends upon which book you read.

If anger is a 'two-edged sword' that cuts both ways, then what is forgiveness? A butter knife that 'spreads' both ways?

It felt good to heal myself, to have dug down deep into my sub-conscious and to bring out those very critical moments that brought about my self-inflicted pain. To look at those moments, feel the pain all over again and then gently release it.

After my regression, I studied my skin every day, as the therapist said it would improve. It was not as bad as in my childhood and teenaged years, but bad enough at times to prevent me from swimming in a public pool or prancing around in shorts. I do wear long shorts in the summer but the worry of people staring at my obvious imperfection has continued to cause me embarrassment. Most often people are too preoccupied to take notice of others but even that understanding does little to still the fluttering of my heart.

The possibility of fleshly freedom is an overwhelming idea. To be free of the 'misery of psoriasis' is daunting. The infliction has been my comfort, my mainstay and my reason for being for so long, it would be difficult to just suddenly wake up and voila! gone forever.

I used to wonder why I was the only one in my family who was burdened with this misery for all to see. Why me? So many nights praying to be 'normal'. And yet, the possi-

bility of my prayer being answered – not only through the Creator, but also myself – is a wondrous idea to conceive.

My sons and Gil have loved me no matter how spotty my skin. Even my first husband was never bothered by it. Just me – ***I*** *was always bothered. I loathed my body and hence, myself. I did not deserve the good things that life offered. The regression helped me understand a great deal, helped me understand how important forgiveness is for the soul*

One step at a time. Even though I feel that things have shifted inside me, a little skeptic is in perpetual mental residence and loudly proclaims wondrous happenings as unrealistic and impractical.

However, my regressions **were** *wondrous happenings because I began to feel lighter, stronger. I am lighter because I released the burden of my anger towards my mother and father. I feel stronger because I released the burden of anger towards myself.*

Even if my skin condition persists, the shift has occurred. My soul is not as wary, as fearful that people will discover I am a fraud when I turn up my sleeves or roll up my pant legs. Spots, she has spots! So what...

CUENCA

After spending a week in Huanchaco, we decided to head north to Cuenca, Ecuador. We rode the night bus from Trujillo to the border of Peru and Ecuador, which took about 11 hours. The bus broke down three times. Our fellow travellers, all natives, were very nonchalant and, when the last breakdown occurred in the early morning hours near Tombes (the town just before the border), most of the passengers got off the bus and headed to the sandy hills to do their morning constitutional. (For a South American to be without their supply of toilet paper is 'un-constitutional'.)

At Agua Verdes, Peru, the fun began. Chicanery and bribery is rife here. The two men who took us to the border in the moto-taxi were in cahoots with the Peruvian *Policia* and while we waited to get through the lineup, we were treated to smiles and thinly veiled threats. Gil stood his ground and demanded to know the name of the Officer, demanded to see his Superior. They tried to wear us down but Gil refused to pay any bribe and threatened to report the offence to the Ministry of Tourism. (I knew, but they didn't, that Gil could wear anybody down.) They let us go.

Our two escorts came across with us and insisted on carrying our luggage. Keeping up a fast pace, they led us through a maze of a marketplace covered in tarps. They warned us to keep our backpacks in front for fear thieves would slash them from behind. We were convinced they had led us in circles, but could not prove it and felt angry at our helplessness, our dependence upon their so-called guidance. Finally, we arrived at the bus station and the female clerk told us we had to go back to Ecuadorian immigration to get our papers stamped. The two men demanded another bribe, so Gil handed them a U.S. one-dollar bill. They laughed and demanded more.

We had been travelling all night, our bus had broken down three times, bribes were demanded of us by the Peruvian police, we had been pushed and prodded, led by the nose and now... I was so tired and fed up, I handed them a five-dollar bill just to get the episode over with. They handed the money over to the ticket lady, who verified it was bona fide; they laughed and ran off. Gil lectured me on my bad move.

We took a taxi to immigration and the driver asked us how we liked Ecuador, so far.

We had a few hours until our bus, so we found an open-air restaurant and ordered *almuerzo*. The young man serving us looked achingly like my youngest son, Mark. Even though he lived three thousand miles away from me in Canada, I missed him more in South America. It was hard to tell whether he was the owner's son. I wondered,

Is this his whole life, working in this restaurant? Did he go to school, was there any promise of a good life for him? If I'd had the money, I would have taken that young man and offered to pay his way into a better life. He was dressed in clean blue jeans, T-shirt, sandals and a baseball cap perched backwards on his head. He worked steadily, was unperturbed, even when two office workers impatiently stomped off when they were not served immediately. I wanted to leave him a big tip but knew Gil would not approve, especially after the episode with the two tricksters.

That young man represented a longing in me. In effect, he represented the *'me'* that harbored so many hopes and dreams when I was young. When I stood on the edge of my life and could see to the horizon of wishes fulfilled, dreams realized and a happiness I had never known. I wanted to guide that young man and make sure he avoided all the pitfalls that a gullible and naïve nature created. To be innocent and unprepared for life can be like a deer in the forest facing down the barrel of a gun for the very first time. Surreptitiously, I left a good-sized tip and we ran to catch our bus.

The bus ride to Cuenca was another four hours and without incident. The trip through the Andes would have been very harrowing except I had left my fear behind in

Agua Verdes. I decided, 'It's in God's hands.' Often you are perched just above precipices that fly straight down, never ending. If I died while the bus passed another bus on the steep, twisting roads, then it was meant to be. I drowsed and dozed.

We arrived in Cuenca at about 8 o'clock in the evening and a man and woman approached us as we got off the bus and offered to take us to their hostel, *Los Americanos*. We looked at their brochure and it sounded like a good deal so we climbed into their Ford Explorer and off we went.

The suite was very modern with a large room that gave onto a busy street, with a lot of washing on the line in the yard below. The bathroom was marble with a shower, pedestal sink and a toilet. The rent was $20. U.S. a night, much more than we'd paid in Huanchaco ($5./night). After unloading our suitcases, and having a nap, we went out to explore the streets.

Cuenca's population is about 300,000, and it's the third largest city in Ecuador with an altitude of about 2500 meters. It is a rich, colonial city and the section we walked through looked to be upper-middle-class. High, wrought-iron fences and wrought-iron grilles on the windows protected the homes, while vicious guard dogs snapped menacingly at us as we strolled by. A Rottweiler smashed against the fence, its teeth bared, saliva spewing from its angry maw as we passed an apartment complex complete with a security guard and small sentry station. I wondered where the land mines were located.

As in most South American cities, the car is king, so you have to take your life into your hands when you cross the street. Count to ten, take a deep breath, hold hands and run like frightened jackrabbits. Sometimes both my feet left the ground when Gil pulled me across a Cuencan street.

The colonial, 'old town' part of Cuenca is quite lovely. Lots of markets, cobbled streets, cafés, restaurants – yet horrendous traffic belching diesel fumes. The next morning we met a couple from Ottawa who had just returned from the Galapagos Islands. We ran across the street and exclaimed, "White folks!" Not just the colour of skin but somebody who speaks English, what a thrill.

My first view of Cuenca was a lovely photo in the 'International Living' magazine. This city particularly and Ecuador in general, are touted as great places to live and also great places in which to invest. The picture looked as if it were taken from either a mountain or an airplane. It looked so colonial, so serene. No diesel-spewing buses in sight. I should have taken a picture of the Rottweiler and sent it to the editors of the magazine.

I was ill for three days. 'Embedded.' I thought I had the flu but later learned it was a bad bout of '*altura*' or altitude sickness. My head throbbed, I threw up and my stomach ached with pain and nausea. Gil went to the *farmacia* (drug store) and got me some stomach pills, anti-nausea pills, vomit pills and anti-bacterial pills. Take these now, take these twenty minutes later. Our misdiagnosis caused me to take a while longer to recover. Gil ordered room service for breakfast and dinner, went exploring on his own and found the closest Internet café. Even worse than the altitude sickness, was the homesickness. I missed the

CUENCA FLOWER MARKET

Island, missed our family and friends. (I'm not much of an adventuress. To be honest, I suck at being an adventurous traveller…)

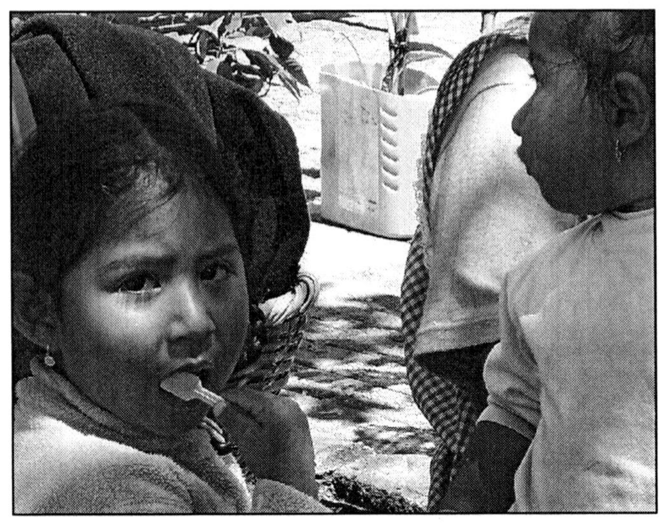

NATIVE GIRLS IN CUENCA MARKET

CUENCA BUS TERMINAL

Our Spanish was coming along nicely, but we couldn't wait to get out of Cuenca because of the noise and air pollution. The churches were extraordinary, though their juxtaposition with the begging poor was a little hard on the heart. And further, these churches were built from the sweat of the working poor. I hope it was worth it.

We talked to a lovely German girl at the hostel and she told us that when crossing the same border as we, she and her friend were held hostage in the *collectivo*, or minibus. They were told that European passports were very valuable on the black market and people would kill for them. They handed over $100. U.S. each, for a bribe and thought they were lucky to escape with their lives. "Isn't it sad?" she commented, "What we will remember about this trip is being terrified out of our wits. What a sad way to remember South America…"

For a few hours, I felt better. We walked the streets but when we got back to the hostel, the illness assailed me anew. I returned to our room and, dropping my clothes, slid beneath the clean sheets. I prayed to the powers-that-be, the one, or ones, controlling our fates, our bodies and some of our actions. I begged them to take the upset away from me.

Then, like a warm band wrapping around my body protectively, I felt relief. Suddenly, wonderfully – no upset stomach, no nausea – all gone. I sent up a prayer of thanks and soon fell blissfully asleep.

LIFE AS A HAYSTACK

We stopped at a roadside inn after a long, grueling car trip on the Island. We were tired, Gil and I, but glad we had made it as far as we had.

The motel room was nicely furnished, clean and very welcoming. After munching snacks from the cooler, we donned our nightshirts and climbed into one of the queen-sized beds and turned on the television.

While Gil surfed channels, I dozed and snuggled down deeper into the blankets. The drone of a legal drama and the protective warmth of my man's body felt like a cocoon. This had to be the most comfortable, warmest place on the whole planet. Suddenly, I was telescoped to a time in my childhood.

My mother worked on a farm picking fruit and since I was too young for school, she had to bring me along with her. I remember she tucked me into a haystack with the sun shining down. It was autumn, I think, as the air was cool, crisp. I felt safe and warm in that haystack, felt nothing could ever harm me. I dozed off and on throughout the morning, and when it was time for lunch, my mother returned with a thermos of coffee and baloney sandwiches wrapped in waxed paper. The coffee was sweet with lots of milk and the taste was as comforting as the place I rested within. Because I was so hungry, the sandwiches tasted like the better side of heaven.

After we ate, my mother returned to work and with my belly full, I contentedly dozed the rest of the afternoon away. I must have been about two or three years old, yet the memory of those sensations stayed with me throughout my life. Now here it was, dovetailing with a present moment. I was the child/wife nestled in a haystack/motel room bed being warmed by the sun-mother-love/protective warmth of my mate. The drone of the insects hovered around me as the drone of the television lulled me deeper into my cocoon.

I think I remember that childhood moment because it was shared only between my mother and me. Being the last of five, I seldom got the chance to experience her particular attention so this was one of only a few. I experienced a gentle tenderness at that time and the warm haystack and the shared lunch heightened every sensation. The feelings matched so well, the haystack and the motel, it was as if the past and the future superimposed themselves upon each other and then – no time.

That it would come to me while dozing in a motel room snuggled warmly against my mate was no surprise. It was our particular love that drew the circle full.

ONWARDS

Initially, Gil and I considered renting an apartment in Cuenca. But unlike the romantic depiction in the periodical, I was not enchanted with the place. The traffic alone was too much. Buses, cars, taxis – never-ending. I found the 'Cuencans' not as polite as the Peruvians, though it was beautiful in the old part of the city. Being typical turistas, we took a lot of pictures, toured the markets and rustic churches. In a way, it was our duty.

I've always admired people who write about their travels and discourse on the history of the area travelled, describe in detail the flora and fauna and wax poetic about museums and galleries. For me, copping abstract info from the 'Lonely Planet' is enough and let's be done with it. I like birds and bushes a whole lot, but not enough to learn the names of every indigenous plant, animal, insect and tree. Well, who really cares, I ask you? My eyes would glaze over in ten seconds flat.

Before leaving Cuenca, we took a bus trip to a few market villages. In many South American towns and/or cities, the bus companies are ubiquitous and all over the map. They are privately owned and you have to go from one to the other to assess their superiority and cost-effectiveness. Many overnight buses or *camas*, are very 'luxe'. They are double-deckers, with seats that convert into beds, a bathroom in the lower deck, offer food and beverages and there is a private TV screen in front of each double seat.

The bus we took from Trujillo to the border was single-decked, with nubby, blue-upholstered seats that either leaned back or didn't, depending upon their maintenance. A single T.V. behind the bus driver blared a Spanish-speaking movie. The movie that played was mainly about a husband/father who drank and beat his wife. Over and over again it played the opening scene of this man coming home after a major bender and smacking the hell out of his long-suffering wife. The DVD would stop after a few more scenes, the assistant to the bus driver would come back and twiddle with the machine, which then started the movie all over again. I got to the point of being so tired and fed up, I actually started rooting for the husband!

However, in Cuenca, the bus station is one huge, marbled beauty. All roads lead to here. The taxi driver dropped us off and we walked into the depot and could not believe our eyes. Relaxed seating everywhere, a food court, clean (pay-as-you-go) bathrooms, and kiosk after kiosk of helpful tour agents. We bought tickets to Gualaceo and Chordeleg markets.

The ride to anywhere you go, whether express or not, is not usually express, save for the most expensive overnight tour buses. Usually there are many, many stops to let on indios, the aboriginal people you see in *National Geographic.* The women are so colourful wearing bright skirts, aprons with fedoras perched jauntily on their heads. There are sometimes large, padded seats behind the drivers and they, their baskets and other paraphernalia, perch there.

Not only local villagers, but food and drink hawkers, get on and off the buses. They sell *empanadas*, (large, deep-fried meat or chicken-filled dumplings), pop, *papas fritas* (french fries), *helado* (ice cream), and homemade popsicles. (We assumed the driver got kickbacks from these sales.) Most often, we passed on the goodies, but found the *empanadas* to be very tasty and bought those for the long trips. Being reserved, private Canucks, we found the constant soliciting, while trying to enjoy the scenery, very annoying. But, being very polite, we smiled and pretended this was a wonderful part of our journey.

We got off first at Gualaceo, along with three tourists from Belgium. Gil was able to use his French and we shared travel tips and places to go. Walking further down the street, we found the huge marketplace. Everywhere you looked there were whole, roasted pigs. You walked up, chose your part and it was whisked onto a paper plate.There were open-air soup kitchens, vegetable stalls and stalls selling just-killed chickens. (These folks certainly were not averse to the sight of blood.)

GUADACEO PIG MARKET

CHORDALEG ZOCALO

CUENCA MARKETPLACE

We shared some homemade soup with the locals and finished off with a coconut concoction like a milkshake. We then boarded another bus to Chordeleg. Suddenly my stomach began to pitch and turn. I knew that the local water in the coconut drink was anathema to my bowels. Jumping off the bus at the main marketplace on the square, we raced around looking for a *baño* or bathroom.

Finally, we found a local bathroom and were so glad we'd learned to keep a good supply of toilet paper. Finished, I went outside to wait for Gil, who had experienced the same bowel issue. The view was beautiful. The village perched on a hill, the verdant mountains stretched beyond and high across the road, a banner of bougainvillea. I casually glanced over by a stone wall and there an Ecuadorian native lady had lifted her skirt and was defecating against the abutment. Good for you, I thought. Au naturel. Standing up, she pulled down her skirt and continued on her way, with nary a glance from the passers-by. Ho-hum, life in the Andes.

Gil bought me a silver ring of my choosing, inscribed with Incan lettering from one of the small shops in the *zocalo* or village square. We've lived together for 10 years and finally something to mark our joining together. I told him, "Now I feel well and truly married to you." Not just married but connected by a symbol of our unity.

CUENCA FLOWER MARKET

LIFE AS A FOOTBALL

After my parents separated, my mother and I moved to the North end of the city into a very small apartment on the top floor of a house. The landlord was cranky but his wife was very nice. though she was too busy producing good, Catholic children to temper his moods.

High school was great; I had good friends and my mother was also busy with her new boyfriend, Mr. W. When she wasn't working hard, cleaning in office buildings, he took up her time, leaving me free to do as I pleased. In my almost-last year of school, my mother decided to move to British Columbia, to live with my eldest sister and her partner. My world fell apart. My mother wanted to escape her boyfriend and I was the sacrifice. I was to be a live-in babysitter for a family friend when I finished the school year.

The plans fell through and two of my friends came forward and offered to let me stay with them. I very much appreciated their kindness but felt I was more a charity case than a guest. These were upper-middle class families and I was from the wrong side of the tracks. I felt like 'Olivia' Twist, though I didn't dare ask for more.

It was the year the astronauts walked on the moon and every face was glued to every T.V. set in North America. One leap forward for mankind, but one step backward for me and my uncertain life. My friend, Janie, came to the rescue and since her parents had long been divorced, her mother very easygoing and often away. We lived like I had lived with my mother, free to do as we pleased.

Mr. W. came to visit me with promises of a real 'family' life. He wanted my mother to return and he knew I was the soft link to secure his agenda. It worked. He, my mother and I moved into a high rise apartment the summer of her return. I was miserable. My skin was so bad, I felt like an ugly lizard.

One night, as I sat with a friend on the balcony, laughing and talking, Mr. W. raced out of the bedroom and screamed at us to get out. We walked several kilometers to her house and I spent the night there. The next day my mother suggested I move out West to live with my eldest sister. And so I did.

The household of my sister and her mate was very uncertain, as well. My sister worked nights as a nurse as well as caring for her own son and her two stepsons. Her relationship with her partner bordered on dismal. One morning, an explosion erupted between her partner and me. I was told to leave. I cried all the way to school. Where to now?

I talked to a fellow student, whose father happened to be a social worker and they placed me in a home in the student-welfare system. I was put in a bedroom with the young daughter and was expected to clean and baby-sit. The kids were spoiled rotten and never listened to me, so I gave up. I phoned my caseworker and when she learned of my situation, promised to get me out of there. "Let me tell them," I said, "or there will be hell to pay." She agreed. I got back to the house and the woman waited at the door with a stick and threatened to beat with me it. "How could you do this to us?" she screamed, "After all we've done for you?" News travelled fast. I stayed in my room until it was time to go.

Finally, I landed somewhere nice and secure. Her name was Mrs. Mulholland, an elderly lady who was kind, funny and intuitive. She and her husband had been in a car accident and he was confined to a care home. Coming home on weekends, he bitched the whole time he was there. Sunday nights after he left were peaceful.

Mrs. Mulholland took me to a doctor and I was put on a diet for my skin – no fried foods, anything with cholesterol in it. My skin cleared and I think it was mainly because I was in a place where I felt wanted. My mother came to visit and we went for a walk. I told her I couldn't count on her, that I didn't need her anymore. I guess I wanted to hurt her, as well as to announce my independence.

I finished school and went back East to live in Toronto. My mother and Mr. W. were living together in his house, so I'd visit them on the occasional weekend. One morning, when my mother went to work, Mr. W. came into my bedroom and crawled in beside me. Realizing his intent, I screamed at him so he got up and told me to go back to my perverted friends in Toronto. I guess that was his idea of a 'real' family.

Looking back, I wonder why I experienced so much back-and-forthing in my life. I felt kicked around like an old worn-out football. As soon as I landed on solid ground, I felt the next boot against my backside and off I sailed again, into the air, never knowing if the next landing would be in a mud puddle, ditch or on a soft, grassy mound. What kind of idiot was I to have helped create this groundless reality?

I knew I fit the two common archetypes of Rebel and Abandoned Child. It was my Rebel that caused my Abandoned Child to be kicked around so much. Yet it was the Rebel that kept me going, kept me fighting to stay sane and alive.

Now into my fifties, I still pine for a home, a place where I feel secure and safe. So much needs fixing and so many empty rooms; what should I fill them with?

PUERTO LOPEZ

Gil and I decided, after talking to a travel agent in Cuenca, to head for Puerto Lopez, a fishing village on the west coast of Ecuador.

The bus ride was exhausting. We had to change buses in Guayakil. The main bus terminal was huge, with about 6 buildings jutting out from the main one, reminiscent of an airport. It was so hot, I wondered if the coast would be as bad. We got lost, so Gil asked a militiaman to help us find our connection. Suffice it to say, we had an 'armed escort' right to our bus. I hadn't had a pee break in several hours and our bus was leaving immediately. To the holding tank it went.

Guayakil, to give a short description, is the business centre of Ecuador. It is teeming, large and from what I saw, dusty and dirty. (We learned there was an American military base located at Masala, several hours north – the only one in Ecuador.) The waterfront had been turned into a tourist attraction but many travellers were not interested enough to get that far. It is mainly a place to pass through for flights to the Galapagos, Quito and other more attractive destinations. And we were two of the ones passing through.

Our next bus change was Saint Helena, a tiny little village about 2 hours from Puerto Lopez. On the way, I sat beside a native woman holding her sweet baby. I gave the child, a girl, a tiny straw basket to play with. Her mother was very reserved, not friendly at all. The child fell asleep on her shoulder and for the better part of that journey I watched, with fascinated delight, the chubby cheeks, the pudgy fingers moving and twitching on the mother's shoulder. The mother held her child with ease and comfort as if she was part of her body and I envied her, as I was a very reluctant and awkward first-time mother, way back when.

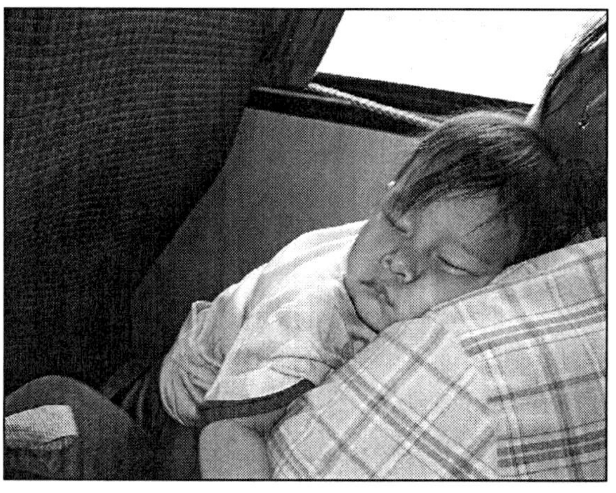

I didn't expect the woman to converse with me, and respected her reserve yet, when we got off to change buses in Saint Helena, she made sure we waited at the correct spot by waving and pointing us in the right direction. No smile, but in some small way she did care.

The bus to Puerto Lopez was packed, really packed. School kids heading to their village homes jammed the aisle from front to back. In many South American buses, not only is there a padded area behind the driver, there is usually a spare seat beside him. Gil sat in that seat while I sat directly behind on the large pad. I was exhausted and my bladder had peaked out in Guayakil. Nodding off, I drowsed for about 40 minutes until the last of the students disembarked.

The scenery was a visual improvement, compared to the desert-like landscape on the northwest coast of Peru. Some of the towns and villages we passed were quaint and picturesque with bougainvillea spilling over white cement walls and the odd palm tree hanging about. I wondered if Puerto Lopez would be like that, quaint and inviting.

We headed up a hill and the descent led to 'our' village. From the top it looked inviting with bright blue and turquoise fishing boats lazing on the water, the ocean waves flashing strongly to the shore. Then we arrived in the centre of the village where it was dusty and dilapidated.

In lieu of taxis, Puerto Lopez use 'moto-taxis', which are merely motorcycles converted to a kind of covered surrey with two wheels in the back. Here the drivers aggressively pester the tourists and soon our suitcases were whipped out from under the buses and transferred to the back of the taxi. (The cost was very expensive – 50 cents…)

The first thing I did when we arrived was race around looking for a bathroom. After hours and hours of travel, my bladder felt numbed by the constant changing of busses, jostling and exhaustion. I raced into a small cantina and 'had it out' with my overfilled organ. The release felt like a full body orgasm. I learned too late, though, that the bathroom had no toilet paper so I rooted in my shoulder bag for some old tissues. No tissue, but a restaurant napkin filled in. Once settled, toilet paper would top our grocery list.

Not many people in Ecuador speak English. Our Spanish, though improved somewhat from Huanchaco and Cuenca, still consisted of 'pidgin' Spanish. Gil's first language is French so his comprehension and grasp of the language is better than mine. Somehow we made it known we needed a hostel/hotel. There was one right in town, very basic, but I needed to be by the ocean. After a few false starts, we found a small hostel, Carlos Alberto, a little way past the *malecon*, or paved road fronting the beach.

For $12. U.S. a night, we got a second-floor corner room, small but clean. The sound of the surf was music to my ears, so much so that I didn't think to ask if the *agua* was *caliente* for our showers. Oh well. At least I began to feel more grounded, less tossed around by the tide of fate.

The owner of our hostel was not Carlos Alberto. (We later learned this was the name of a famous soccer player.) We actually forgot his name after introductions to his wife and two small daughters. So much to take in. The place had been newly constructed and the owner's father-in-law owned a hostel closer to the paved *malecon*. All of the rooms were very small and ours shared a balcony with the one next door. I noticed that the balcony wall was only thigh-high and wondered whether, after a night of too many *cervezas*, some hapless, happy drunk might trip and plunge head-first to the sand below.

We asked if there was a *cocina* (kitchen) we could use but 'Carlos' made it clear only his wife used it. We had no way to brew our own tea or coffee in the morning and our landlord said he would allow that. Just that. We knew we would not be staying here long as the need to spread out, have our very own domestic space and rooms separate from our sleeping area was necessary for our well-being. Gil and I both love to cook and found preparing our own meals a very satisfying and settling experience. We vowed to go apartment hunting the next day.

It was very quiet on this end of the beach. The sounds from the *malecon* were muted and indistinct. Walking hand in hand, we passed what looked like an abandoned fishery. However, we learned, the ocean catch was still cleaned there before being taken to inland villages. It emanated a strong, fishy smell so we passed quickly by. The sand felt warm and comforting beneath our feet and it looked as if efforts were made to keep the beach clean for tourists.

The surf roared and chastened the shore then roared back towards the horizon, only to return full force. I took off my shoes and allowed the rushing water to burble between my toes and squish out mucky sand. It is amazing how a body of water and acres of sand can send one back in time, cause one to feel like a child. If a human cannot comfort, then a sea, a lake or an ocean, can.

We needed to grab some dinner so we strolled toward the restaurants lining the beach. In the distance my eyes caught a familiar sight. It was our friends, Kay and Dan – right here in Puerto Lopez! Rushing towards them, we hugged and exclaimed over the coincidence that brought us all together to this place.

They introduced us to Raoul, their landlord at their hostel, Itapoa, which is listed in the 'Lonely Planet' guidebook. He is an Ecuadorian who lived in New York for several years then came back and married a lovely Brazilian lady named Maria. His English was very good but we were more interested in catching up with our friends, with their adventures so we found a restaurant, ordered *cervezas*, the daily *pescado* (fish) and brought each other up to date.

We had forgotten it was Kay and Dan's intention to come to Puerto Lopez after Huanchaco. After our border experience, my illness in Cuenca and our decision not to remain in that noise-polluted city, Gil and I scoured our guidebooks searching for a quiet place to rest our weary selves. The visit to the travel agent and her description of various cities and villages along the coast firmed our decision. Being here was like travelling full circle.

While we ate our *pescado empanada* (breaded fish) with salsa and sliced avocado, we listened to the ocean and watched the sun set across the busy street. Hazes of amber, gold and streaks of smoky blue attended its descent. Night in Ecuador arrives quicker than the blink of a cat's eye.

We met two Russians from Moscow, Sergei and Alexei, who are air traffic technicians. Their government pays for them to fly anywhere for their holidays and here they were, sitting at the next table sampling *pescado empanada* and *camarones* (shrimp). We shared drinks and comparisons between our respective countries. Sergei was a gentle soul who'd been married for 30 years and Alexei, too, was long married with two adult sons. Later, we met Steve, a young mining engineer, who lived in the States but had actually lived and worked in Russia. I found it strange and so interesting that here, in a small fishing village on the west coast of Ecuador, so many worlds and cultures met and mixed. There was Steve, struggling to recall Russian phrases, two Russians struggling to recall a few English phrases with virtually no Spanish in their repertoire, conversing with four Canadians from the West Coast of

Canada, struggling to recall their limited Spanish.

What is Russia like since the fall of communism? Good for the young, bad for the old. What is Putin like? Well… What about the Russian mafia? Does it run everything – politics and economics? Well… Don't worry, the KGB is no longer listening in. (Unless the Russian government paid for them to fly to Ecuador on an all-expense paid junket.) We took digital photos, hugged and went off to bed in the small room in our hostel with the sound of the surf in our sleepy ears.

FROM RUSSIA WITH LOVE:
SERGEI AND ALEXEI

POOR BIG, RICH GIRL

The hypnotherapist had little difficulty putting me under. Taking what looked like an orange-colored lava lamp, she plugged it in and set it on the table to the left of my chair. My neck stiffened a bit from stretching to turn and look at it, but I couldn't stop from staring into its bright depths. Her voice receded as I began to close my eyes, my breath softening and my heart slowing to a lazy beat. I felt this stranger inside impatiently tapping her toes, imperiously willing me to give free rein to her voice.

The hypnotherapist's leading voice and my too-slow thoughts made her want to jump out, take over and take charge. She was a force to be reckoned with – and she was me. Or, actually, the me I used to be, once upon a time in another life.

"I have a chauffeur who takes me where I want to go in a long, black limousine. The servants do as they are told; I have absolutely no patience with them. I have a temper, I lose it because I can't abide stupidity of any kind. None of them like me at all, but what do I care? They're just servants, after all.'"

I sat there, she took over my psyche and I let her. She rose up and willed me to step aside and because I was a mere subject, I easily gave her center stage. She soon filled it with her selfish, grasping ego. I loved her – had to, because she helped shape me and my spirit, helped me survive this life. I hated her – had to, because she helped cause my skin condition – a curse, a punishment and yet a humble blessing in this life.

She barely tolerated the therapist's questioning, probing voice. My psyche knew that the hypnotist was here to get to the root of my skin problem and though I had been regressed to my birth in this life and experienced my mother's hatred of giving me life, there was more to uncover. And here it was, here was she giving shape and form to a once-lived life of material wealth and a surfeit of love. I had gone back in time to England sometime before the First World War.

"My father is generous, hypocritical and controlling. He humors my need for the latest styles, salon dinner parties and trips to the continent. He opens his wallet as often as he closes his heart.

"My mother is a milquetoast and how can my father tolerate such a useless weakling? After not being able to provide a son and heir – only a headstrong, petulant daughter – he cast her off. And who wouldn't? Really the woman is insufferable."

She wanted to impress the hypnotist with all the opulence of her life. The palatial homes, the jewelry and the young, enthusiastic men standing in line hoping to win her very be-ringed left hand. They wanted the life, to win over her father who held the purse strings. If she married, it was understood her husband would be the one in control of her life and lifestyle. She had so much, but so little. She felt powerless and alone. She loved her father with a fierce, burning hatred.

"Then, like a beacon on a storm-tossed night, he appeared. Blue eyes, dark hair and a big smile, he came to the stables, to the barns, looking to do odd jobs and there were plenty. I kept the regular staff so busy with other chores they have little time, so in a pinch, he can fill in. He is a charming one, that man, and I fell hard."

Her mind bucked and pleaded. It was a secret place the therapist was now probing and she resented the intrusion. Yet, part of her wanted to talk, to brag that someone as handsome as he could want her, a plump, matronly-looking, spoiled brat.

"He looks beautiful in blue; it makes his eyes darker and deeper. Who knew who seduced who, but we made love in the barn on the hay and I loved the feel of him over me, taking me, dominating me. He makes me do things I never would have done with my lazy, rich beaus. But because I want him, don't want to lose him, I comply. And oh, how I love it – the secrecy, the passion, his swarthy, hot body – and just the thought that my father would hate this makes me love him all the more.

"I love his Irish brogue and the way he pinches my plump body and says, 'What foin hips ye have fer birthin', me girl, fer bearin' me bairn.' And I know that was all I would ever want for the rest of my life: to be his wife, give him children and care for us forever, wherever or whatever. Proud and penny foolish, but so what?"

Her voice lowered; she could barely reveal what happened next. It was shameful, but needed to be told, so the one in this life could heal. She would tell even if it would kill her, but really it already had. She was not going to let what happened punish the one who sat in the chair in the therapist's office.

"My father discovered us. Who knew how long he knew; it wouldn't have surprised me if he had watched us for a long time as we rutted in the hay in the barn. I knew, without really knowing, that the stablemen had tipped him off. They all hated me anyway so it was a matter of time. And maybe, just maybe, I wanted the truth to finally come to light. Or maybe, in some perverse way, I enjoyed the idea of being caught out by that miserable, old man.

"My clothes were half-off. I can't recall if we were done our lovemaking or just beginning. My lover was pulled off me and sent off with a beating and many fierce kicks to his backside. I never saw him again after that. But the rest is scored in my memory forever.

"That cruel, sadistic man paraded me past the servants, refused to let me cover myself, and I was forced, red-faced, with my clothes hanging off my body, to walk a gauntlet. Up the steps, through the marble halls and up the long staircase to my bedroom. My father followed me, smirking and berating me the whole, endless time. I knew he was cruel, knew he was ruthless, but never knew its extent. The humiliation, the abasement did not end there. Oh God, how could I say the rest?"

The therapist would not leave her alone until she told the rest of the whole, sordid tale.

The tears flowed unchecked down her face, the sobs heaved the body of the present 'she' and the past 'she', the pain now shared.

"There in my opulent, spoiled bedroom my father raped me, his one and only daughter. Defiled and desecrated, my mortal body and immortal soul. The brand of his filth, his incestuous, odious filth seared me and bound him to me in a way no one would ever know. And where was God when this was happening? Probably paid off for keeping His mouth shut by my wealthy, powerful father. I wouldn't have been surprised at all.

"He called me a slut; I knew I was but to make my punishment complete, he pushed me down on my bed and rammed inside me, pinning me down with his strength, his hatred and his jealousy. Yes, he was jealous because

my father owned everyone and everything, and anyone who dared to trespass on his property suffered his endless wrath. I must have fainted, blacked out, because when I awoke he was gone.

"Yes, yes my clothes grew tighter; the dressmaker chided me for eating too many desserts, but that wasn't it"

She felt her skin expand, as she sat there with her eyes closed. She saw herself bent over the porcelain bowl in the morning as she heaved out her insides. She hoped the child was her lover's, wanted desperately to believe their love rose above everything, even the filthy act of her father. Yet she knew with an all-God knowing that the seed of her father dominated and won out. It was to be his child and grandchild.

"After the birth, they took it away, I didn't care, didn't see it, didn't ask its sex, nothing mattered anymore. I felt numb, had been for a very long time. I succumbed just as my mother did, and I understood. My father was in the business of breaking spirits and whoever my mother was before, she was now bent and wasted. Now so was I.

"I married the first man who came along. Someone kind, easily manipulated by my father. He was also plump, and we grew plumper together. Eating was my only pleasure. The pies, the cakes, filled the empty, bottomless crevasse inside of me. I shoveled it in, it went down, down and I never felt full, filled, fulfilled. Never.

"Yes, I had children – two boys who, for a time, filled my life and I loved them. There was a nursery, a school-house, but father took them under his wing, said he would see to their education. After all, they were the hope of the future. But no, he stole my light all over again, punished me for my deceit and I let him. The numbness set in and the food was all life was worth.

"I still treated the staff badly but this time, I was in my own home. At least the home my father bought when he bought my obsequious husband. And who could blame him? It was a good life; we got along fine, always separate bedrooms. He could find his own outside comforts just as long as he let me be. He was a good man that way and by all rights, I was lucky."

As if from a distance I could hear the voice of the therapist take me/her to the last day of my/her life.

"I grew so fat. My hair is grey but finely curled and combed. The housekeeper kindly placed a feather in my hair, the way I liked to wear it when I was young. I probably looked foolish, but it gives me a lift somehow. I am alone, my husband long gone. My sons are long gone as well, strangers to me – all due to my father. He bought them off, too.

"I am dying of all the diseases associating with eating too much and eating all the sweet, fat things that comforted to kill me. Diabetes, heart disease, clogged blood ves-

sels – all of that. I am alone, was always so alone. There are the marble floors, of course, and the servants. I even let them bring their children around to use the nursery and the schoolhouse. I wanted to hear their voices, so alive and full of life. I must have learned to be kinder to my staff because they were the only ones by my side when I passed on. My father, the old bastard, was long gone but his ghost was always there to haunt and punish me. I never really owned a damned thing in my life. I had nothing, was nothing and I passed into nothingness. How he wanted it!"

The tears fell anew and the therapist brought me slowly back to the present and placed a box of Kleenex in my lap. I gazed at it for a while then slowly pulled out a tissue. My nose felt congested from all the crying throughout the session. I imagined how ridiculous I looked with my mucous-filled nostrils. She must have witnessed this soul-bearing desecration a thousand times before. God bless her patience. I saved the best for last.

My therapist asked me what was the source of my present-day skin condition? Even before she ended her question, she interrupted with the answer.

"I was allergic, you see. Allergic to the hay we made love upon. We made love in the hay and I was severely allergic. My body used to break out in great red welts and after my father found us, shamed me and defiled me, he always taunted me by saying, 'My dear, you really must stay away

from the barn. You know how you react to the hay, really a most painful sight, you know.' He never let me forget, even when he was an old, doddering idiot and I a fat matron, miles past the idea of hiding in lofts, slaking my misbegotten passion with a man of odd jobs."

The session was over but her aura lingered on. I knew she was me, seamlessly me, but my conscious mind refused to accept I'd been such a person. Someone selfish, spoiled, prone to tantrums, a snob, cruel to those considered of lesser station. And needy, endlessly needy. She must have been a leech to her so-called friends currying their disinterested favor with gifts and promises of more to come. I felt repulsed by such a person but knew it was time to bring her to my heart, embrace her and soothe away her hurts, her anguished soul.

I know who my father was in that life. He was a friend I had trusted. When my marriage came apart, I turned to him for kindness and nurturing, and he turned on me with cruelty. I also knew that members of my present-day family were part of my staff then and were subjected to the pointed ends of my cruelty. I understood why they looked for ways of 'getting back' at me. After my regression, I no longer felt resentment, hurt or anger anymore – because I knew why. And the odd-job man? That was Gil. I knew that right from the beginning.

I learned that in re-living past lifetimes, we often return in subsequent incarnations with the same people. Not only that, our roles change continuously as if we're acting in a new play. I discovered that my eldest son had been my father, husband, brother and friend in different incarnations. As for Gil, how many roles will he play with me? What kind of lessons do we need to learn in order to live together harmoniously?

When we parted, the hypnotherapist asked me who I thought the child was, the one I bore with my father and never really saw. I thought immediately of my younger son, Mark. I felt protective of him but couldn't understand him. It made sense, resonated with me. I gave this lady a big hug and went home to my man.

SETTLING IN

Kay and Dan had a line on an apartment. They wanted to get settled in for the Christmas season, and we felt carried along with their plans to be in one place for the approaching celebrations. It was the first week of December, my first Christmas away from my friends and family, in such a faraway land.

What would it be like during the season in this fishing village in Ecuador? For Gil, not a problem, as his sense of wanderlust kept him grounded and interested wherever he roamed. Yet, I felt lonely, even with our friends, even with Gil always with me. He knew how homesick I felt, how much I missed my son, Rob, in Vancouver and our friends on the Island. What he didn't know, was that this trip to South America had shaken my foundation and was challenging me to face a lot of memories and demons I kept hidden from him and even hidden from myself. I sat curiously before a Pandora's box as my left hand warred with my right to keep from opening it.

Kay and Dan had an appointment with Giuseppe, a young transplant from Italy. They were slated to view the top floor apartment of a house he owned. They viewed it, met us for lunch and said they had taken the place, planned to move in the next Monday. Gil and I had gone to the other end of the beach and viewed a quiet, lovely hostel with a deck, common room and shared kitchen for $12. U.S. a night. (We were paying that for just our tiny room.) Our friends had kindly booked us to see the apartment below theirs. However it contained no fridge or stove and we dearly desired our own *cocina* in which to cook the fish newly arrived from the ocean.

We had also asked one of the local fishermen if he knew of a house for rent and Winston Churchill (no kidding…) said he would meet us in the early afternoon. He was taking our two Russian friends out on a fishing expedition and, as it turned out, didn't make it for our rendezvous. We waited over an hour, then gave up. Hopefully the apartment on the *lomo Italiano* (Italian hill) might meet our needs if, as our friends said, Giuseppe would spring for the appliances.

MOTO-TAXIS – PUERTO LOPEZ

We took a moto-taxi to meet our potential landlord. No, it wouldn't be feasible for a fridge and stove to be installed. Too costly, if we were only staying a month. We could share facilities with our friends, but all of us vetoed that idea. Besides we had a place down by the ocean waiting for us, so prepared to take our leave.

Wait, Giuseppe called and in Spanish, Italian and mangled English, explained that his uncle had an apartment for rent. Renato owned the large house down the hill. (An Italian couple with two young children had rented his other house in between.) We trudged down the hill to take a look. Renato's house was comprised of four apartments, two on each side, the right side partially on basement level. There were two larger, inner apartments with separate balconies, totally furnished. We viewed the

OUR PUERTO LOPEZ 'VILLA'

apartment, which shared a wall with Renato's place. He was asking $250. U.S. for the month. The kitchen was adequate and the view of the distant hills and the ocean side was lovely. But wait. Renato offered to move out of his place to the next-door suite and rent his place for $300. U.S. per month. We walked in and Gil said, "I'll pay the extra 50 bucks to stay here!"

It was huge, with tiled floors, high ceilings, a master bath with double sinks, a terraced balcony, capacious shower and a Jacuzzi tub (but no fixtures…).

The kitchen was perfect for our needs. There was a curved, wooden counter with high-backed stools, a long wooden counter for food preparation and a six-burner gas stove. The fridge was very large with a good-sized freezer. We took it and arranged to move in two days hence, on a

FISHERMEN ON BEACH IN PUERTO LOPEZ

Thursday. Finally, a place in which to settle and feel human again.

Puerto Lopez is a fishing village but also sells tours to the Isla de la Plata, which advertises itself as a mini-Galapagos but, we've heard, a dismally disappointing one. From April to September, tourists pour in for the whale watching but after that the whales move farther north-west to cooler waters, towards the Galapagos Islands. In December, the tourist season is quite flat, though the fishing is still productive. The tour operators approach the tourists when they arrive but not with a great deal of enthusiasm. Once we settled in, we were virtually left alone.

EMAIL TO FRIENDS AND FAMILY - December 11/06

Dear All:
We have been in Puerto Lopez almost a week and are decompressing from being on the road so much, in Peru and Ecuador. We have rented a sort of 'villa' on a hill overlooking the harbor and it is very spacious and comfy. We spend our days shopping for our daily meals, reading, napping and sometimes bussing to neighboring villages, towns and cities. The Internet is very bad here and expensive. It is dial-up and often down, what a pain, but go with the flow. Our good friends from BC, Kay and Dan, have rented a house higher up our hill and it is nice to have people to schmooze and hang out with. We are planning on taking a bus to a more northern city, Portoviejo, to shop for Christmas. It is hard to get a lot of things we take for granted like wine glasses, towels and even ground coffee. Nary a coffeemaker in sight, just drink a lot of tea. The main tea here is called 'Hornymans, easy to remember. We eat a lot of fish but the chicken is very expensive, about a dollar a pound and the 'gallinas' are very stringy. For Christmas Eve we are having lobster and then a large chicken for

> Christmas Day. After the first week of January it is back on the road again. The people are friendly and crime is almost non-existent in this small village of about 3,000. We get homesick at times – well, I get homesick all the time – so send us an email now and then to let us know how and what you are doing. Though we are very near to the Equator, it is not as hot as you would imagine. The wet season is in January and we will wait and see how that is. Take care and write soon.

That was on the outside. Two adventurous travelers, living in a villa on the hill in a picturesque fishing village on the west coast of Ecuador. How perfect, and so National Geographic meets *International Living*. But the reality was not so happy. Gil discovered how cheap beer was (55 cents a pint) and began his happy hour earlier and earlier in the day. We read a lot and argued more. Gil and Dan had been friends for about 30 years and had never resolved their issues with each other. Kay had said how happy she was to have a female friend but the promise of our own just-girls outings never materialized.

I ached for my Island home, could not keep my spirits up even though envious friends in the colder Northwest wrote emails to say how lucky we were, how exciting it must be to be in such an exotic, faraway land. The truth was, I would have been happy to trade it all in, just to be back where I belonged, no matter how wet or windy or cold.

I felt restless and needed to challenge my mind so I began to decode the Spanish newspapers. Sitting at the dining table every day with the Spanish/English dictionary, I slowly and tediously began to attempt to translate the news. However, this and the three daily walks into town alongside the chickens, donkeys and mangy mutts plus cooking, and reading, could not stem the tide of homesickness. Gil did his best to try to dispel my melancholy but his drinking was also getting me down.

Every few days he would do a water and beer run with Giuseppe in his Jeep. He might as well have filled the water jugs with beer and that would have been his water. We had brought our problems to South America and there was no letting up. The ironic thing was that my skin had cleared up and I could walk freely with shorts and bare legs.

But that was not enough. Finally, I had enough.

I told Gil I planned to leave for Quito and take the next flight home to Canada. I slept that night in the spare room and felt a new determination rise up within me. I could do this, I knew I could. I woke up calm and clear-eyed. Gil approached me in the kitchen.

"If I quit drinking, do you think it will make a difference in our relationship?"

"Well, yes, of course."

"All right, then. I'll quit right now, and then will you stay until we leave together?"

"Of course, I'm willing to try that." And so we did.

We stayed until January 6th, brought in the New Years'

with Dan and Kay. They planned to stay until the end of March and I wondered how they would fill their time.

The interesting thing about Christmas in Puerto Lopez was, it was business as usual. We thought that being Catholics, they would close up early on Christmas Eve and that Christmas Day in the village would be quiet and still. But no, all the businesses and restaurants remained open, save for the bank.

Walking the *malecon*, we witnessed a very strange sight. There on a hammock sat a chicken. But it wasn't perched there as if on a fence. Like an old lady it pushed the hammock, its neck keeping a steady rhythm as if comforting itself. It ignored us as we watched it swing back and forth, back and forth, its lidless gaze directed out towards the ocean. We looked over to where a native gentleman was relaxed on his own hammock and he laughed out loud at our amazement. We cursed our luck not having our camera but how can you capture such a unique scene in a snapshot? Something to tell the kids and grandkids. Nah, they wouldn't believe it…

New Year's found the natives in a self-induced stupor. We walked the village expecting the same industry as Christmas but this time the citizens, especially the men, were sprawled over tables, on the ground or lying on the side of the street. They called out friendly, drunken greetings to us and we laughed as we walked past.

Throughout the season, we were subjected to the loud music of some of the townsfolk down below the hill. The noise beat an incessant cacophony in our ears while we tried to sleep. Sometimes it would go on the whole night through. On one of our walks, we tried to discover its source. We passed by a tiny shack and an old Ecuadorian lady stood by the fence, as modern English and Spanish carols reverberated, almost shaking down the ramshackle walls. We had no idea if she was the one 'sharing' her Christmas cheer with the rest of the village or was merely a relative. She grinned sheepishly at us, an imperturbable expression on her wrinkled face. She was either deaf or had stuffed chicken feathers in her ears. If anything could send us packing, this was it.

Well, not just that. Directly above us and between our place and Kay and Dan's, was another house, rented by a family from Italy. They had a baby girl and a two or three-year old boy. Every night and during the day, the baby screamed and it was not the wail of a hungry child or a child with a dirty diaper. It was more of a 'bitchy' scream and not only that, the mother was a screamer, too. We could hear her yelling, "Basta, basta!" at her husband or her little boy, who usually minded his own business by playing quietly at the back of the house. One day, the family minus the father, went away on an overnight trip and the whole time they were gone, he put the radio on very loud, drank a lot of beer, danced and laughed himself silly, as he swung gleefully in the hammock. No screaming baby or bitchy wife. The next day, the screamers returned. I never heard a peep out of the husband.

It was time to move on. We bought tickets for a night bus to Quito.

FISH MARKET, PUERTO LOPEZ BEACH

QUITO

What can I say about Quito? To begin with, this city was not particularly in our travel plans. We experienced aspects of Lima, Peru and Cuenca, Ecuador. We passed through the swelter of Guayakil and we thought, "Why bother with another teeming, noisy city?"

For me, Cuenca was a disappointment because I had been ill there, because it was not as peaceful as I had expected and I was not peaceful. It was urban, noisy and though the old town was lovely with its flower markets, cathedrals, cafés and multiple hostels, it did not work its magic on me.

We thought Quito would be a stimulating change from the mind-numbing ennui of Puerto Lopez. Soon enough, we discovered how right we were.

The overnight bus took nine hours but somehow, it went very fast, a precursor of our time in Quito.

We arrived in the city about 6:30 a.m., found a cab, told the driver to take us to our first choice in the Lonely Planet guidebook. Shiny, terra cotta tiles led up to *Hostal L'Auberge.* A man was hosing down the stairway and he was the one who checked us in. The hostel housed a café, an Internet room, reception and these opened onto a courtyard in the back, lined with plants on the stairways and all around. We were shown to a third-floor room with a balcony view that gave onto the modern buildings of Quito proper and the verdant mountains beyond.

Shedding our luggage, we began exploring.

There are many parks in Quito, which makes it more inviting to travellers. (I did not see too many in Cuenca,

STREET SCENE IN OLD TOWN, QUITO

but I am sure they were there somewhere.) In one, a river ran through it, where people peddled small boats with their feet. Nearby was a restaurant where the locals gathered so we joined them and ordered our *desayuno* (breakfast). It consisted of cheese melted in a grilled bun, *jugo* (juice), *huevos revueltos* (scrambled eggs) and coffee and the bill totalled 1.50 USD.

It's not easy being a coffee drinker in Peru and Ecuador. Unless you go to a specialty café, you are usually going to get Nescafe' with *agua caliente* (hot water) or *leché caliente* (hot milk). At home we were accustomed to coffee made from ground, roasted beans – something to roll out of bed for. It's really difficult to get enthused about Nescafe'. I'm sorry, I tried but it didn't happen. A real 'lunchbag letdown' when it comes to breakfast.

We walked Quito for a few hours, even checked out other hostels to compare prices but they didn't have the same ambience as L'Auberge. The cheaper places were about $10. – $13. U.S. a night (Ecuador is tied to the U.S. Dollar) but for $17. we got a beautiful view, Internet and the pleasure of connecting with other travellers.

The city is very clean, either by daily street cleaners or an educated population. In Lima, refuse clogs the streets and sidewalks along with wandering, mangy dogs that leave their particular brand of territorial markings everywhere. Here, there was little or no evidence of either filth.

I thought there would be more white faces in Quito but perhaps the ex-patriots were hiding out from we ignorant gringos, and who could blame them? Sometimes our presence invited smiles of welcome from the citizens, other times it caused frowns but most often, the street hawkers were very glad to see you. Not to mention the occasional

GIL AND 'FRIEND' IN OLD TOWN, QUITO

potential thief, who might follow an ignorant tourist for blocks. (We kept our passport, cash and credit cards in our zipped body wallets.)

Quito is divided into Old Town and New Town, with the *Mariscol Sucré* district a form of division between. Many have referred to the latter area as 'Backpackers Paradise' as it is rife with hostels, Internet cafés and cheap restaurants. You will see more white faces there than anywhere else.

There are so many European travellers in South America. The Euro is higher than the U.S. Dollar, so they are able to get more value than we Canucks. Back in 2000. then-President Noboa hooked up with the U.S. Dollar in order to stabilize the economy and from what we have seen, it works. Rarely did we see many fellow Canadians but a multitude of French, Belge, Swiss, Scandinavian and German travellers.

The Europeans are amazing. When they learn a language, they seem to absorb it like sucking a milkshake from a straw. While sitting with German backpackers, they spoke to their companions in their native tongue, turned to us and spoke impeccable English, then ordered food or conversed with the natives like natives. Europe is so multi-cultural and multi-lingual, the opportunity is there to pick and choose any tongue they like. Still, I admired and envied their determination and discipline in taking on new languages.

I was enchanted with Quito; the energy so alive. The hostel stimulated me like a bracing cup of 'real' coffee and I realized what I lacked in Puerto Lopez was the constant interaction with fellow travellers. I loved exchanging ideas, exchanging stories about similar places we had visited. Also, everything about Quito spoke to me in a whole, new way. Suddenly, finally, I felt as if the ground beneath my feet matched my soul.

Gil says, and I believe him, that it is difficult to get lost in Quito. It is a long city with the higher, greener mountains on the west side and the lower ones on the east.

We hopped a bus (25 cents) to go to a trendy, large mall called El Jardin. Here is where well-heeled Ecuadorians go to shop. We sat at the food court and watched them ascending and descending the escalator. The young women wore spiked heels, perfect makeup and very expensive leathers and blue jeans, while the young men basically wore hip-hop clothing – draggy blue jeans, chains, t-shirts and expensive running shoes. Well-tailored businessmen walked around with briefcases and the older women echoed the clothing style of their younger gender. We got bored after about fifteen minutes. The idea of encountering the North American equivalent of yuppies with more money than brains, was as appealing as Nescafé in the morning.

Just to get in a little education, we walked across to the *'Museo Ecuatoriano de Ciencias Naturales'* (Ecuador's Natural Science Museum). For two dollars (USD) each, we toured through various rooms viewing indigenous butterflies, spiders, bats and the bones of pre-historic mammoths. I got the impression that the scientist who discovered a particular species, probably translated the descriptions using only a dictionary because the English was like chopped suey.

It made me sad because we were the only ones visiting the place and the money realized went towards preserving the species and the environment from whence they came. What a topsy-turvy world we live in. We try hard to promote technology but if there is no chain of nature, no water and food, then the result is 'Global Warming' with escalation of hurricanes, tsunamis, floods and mudslides. What are we going to plug our computers into then - a volcano?

According to Kay and Dan's landlord, Raoul at Hostel Itapoa, Ecuadorians denuded a great deal of their country in the last several years for the sake of greed, usually from multinational corporations. Puerto Lopez was once verdant with many trees, grasses and waterfalls, but all that is gone now. Greed stole the rain forests, so *Norte Americanos* can have their Big Macs and heart attacks. Many indigenous tribes were driven deeper into the rainforests, were killed or driven to oblivion. Thankfully (I'm being facetious here) the tourist industry offers treks into the jungle to visit still-existing 'indio' villages. Raoul said there are eco-stations that take volunteers from all over the world and teach preservation of the land and surviving tribes. I think perhaps that may be too little/too late, but hopefully this may represent the de-progression of global warming and its greedy, grasping causes.

In the museum, they also showed samples of lava from various volcanoes. The closest volcano to Quito is Pichicha on the western side with two summits. Gil and I visited a live volcano in Nicaragua in 1998. Inside deep holes lived parakeet-like birds, that were actually able to breathe the carbon monoxide fumes and survive. (I wonder how they'd survive in Los Angeles…) We felt a tour to another volcano would be redundant and besides that, thieves were known to hang around the paths leading to the summit. Of course I had no worries with Gil. He would have asked for their identification and demanded to talk to their superiors…

REPAIRS WHILE U WAIT, QUITO

CATHEDRAL

UNDERSTANDING

Someone once told me that when you hit the wall, you no longer fight; you give way or give up, then finally allow the currents of life to take over. It gets easier because you stop fighting – yourself or others – and you wonder why you let yourself get so far in, to begin with. To put yourself through so much, beating yourself over the head emotionally and mentally, until the physical body cries 'foul', makes you so ill, you have no choice but to surrender. From whatever ailment you summon, you discover a new perspective and in effect, the illness is a transformative gift – like a diamond with a thousand differing facets. You gaze at it from every angle and learn there are so many ways to look at a thing.

After my regression, my skin experienced an improvement. Not major but definitely a marked change. At about the same time, Gil and I were forced to ferry to the mainland from our Island home for business. I sat and wrote my healing experience down during the entire sea journey. I was so focused, nothing existed – not the ship I was travelling on, not the people around me, not even my husband.

I understood so much from that past lifetime, so much of the 'whys' and 'wherefores'. It all made so much sense, even the reason why, when we made love, I pictured or fantasized us coupling in a barn on a bale of hay with the nickering of horses in the dark distance.

I understood why I forgave my father for his abuse of his children in this life. I used to think, "Well, at least he never sexually abused us." Why would I think that? In that previous life, my father raped me after discovering my lover and me. I knew that the abuse had not started there but was probably an ongoing pattern of cruel incest from when I was younger.

In that life, my sisters were my staff and often subjected to my tempestuous cruelty. I understood why, in this lifetime, they looked for reasons to team up against me, as if familial safety in numbers made their personal criticisms more real and justified. While I understood, forgave and asked for a soul-to-soul forgiveness in return, the ego consciousness continued to rise up and toss out questions. Questions like: What if I had fabricated the regression to create a tool to rid me of the demons of worthlessness? A neat Band-Aid to place upon the knee of my inner suffering child as a way of saying, "There, there now, isn't that better? No more boo-boo – all healed and gone away." What if, what if...

Psoriasis, according to doctors, is a mysterious skin condition. In all the medical journals, magazines and nutrition books, very few health professionals or researchers can pinpoint the actual cause of such a physical punishment. For me, it truly was a punishment and since I was the only one in my family 'bad' enough to catch it, I internalized the outside to the inside, as my penance.

Adolescence was hell. I confided to my husband that I never knew the freedom of wearing a two-piece bathing suit at the beach in the sixties, never knew what it was like to be groped in the back seat of a car by a testosterone-loaded male, while watching the 'submarine races' down by the canal after a school dance. I wouldn't allow any guy close enough for fear he might feel the rash on my neck, my back and on the rest of my body.

I remember, as a child, being asked to leave a public swimming pool because I might be 'contagious'. I walked home and cried and cried. Of course, I never returned to that pool or any other, for many, many years. The humiliation branded my psyche and even after I married, bore children and experienced an overall improvement on my body, the scars remained.

The regression explained so much to me. Not only that we are ongoing spiritual beings, having the occasional physical experience, but that wounds are ongoing, too. What do we need to learn from it all?

I learned that the ego must give way. That imperious, spoiled, ruined girl needed to learn humility. Even in this life, my pride and stubbornness governs me. How long will it take, how many lifetimes before I figure it out? Not too many, I hope. I plan to come back to this planet one more time as a gorgeous, coloratura opera singer and I promise I won't behave like a spoiled diva.

Clarity

Tears alter perception;
Blooms on the sill brighten
And shiver in a clearer light;
Movements are new, precise,
The lift of a hand,
The tilt of a curious face;
Eyes rolled up in laughter
The screen of envy and hate
Drawn quickly down
A bitter disguise pasted
Neatly in its place
I see them all – my vision, my soul
Miss not a thing, not even
The inches of sorrow deftly
Warily, snaking up my spine
And I learn, I learn
Sadness is my eyes
When my body can't turn

LADIES FROM WISCONSIN

After leaving the park, we took the bus and got off around the *Mariscol Sucré* district. There we found an indigenous market where ladies dressed in long black skirts, embroidered blouses, some with babies slung on their backs in wool shawls, sold their wares. We found inexpensive shawls, *camisetas* (t-shirts) and wraps to take home as gifts. I bought a chocolate-colored cambric peasant skirt and Gil bought a Panama hat and a cheap watch from a street vendor.

Going about the market, we kept meeting up with the same woman. Every time we passed her, we'd share comments, then continue on our shopping way. Finally, I ran into this lady one more time, while Gil was off buying his watch. We began a 'real chat' when I asked her where she was from (Texas, but originally Wisconsin). Her name was Dixie Amery. She had short, ash-blonde hair and an open face expressing a fun-loving personality. I told her about our hostel, she told me about hers. I told her the name of our hostel and she pulled out a business card. She was staying at the L'Auberge! Dixie was concerned about finding her way back to the hostel and I offered to escort her back with Gil. (If it was just her and me, it would be the blind leading the blind but, in Gil, we had an excellent guide.) So, after purchasing a Panama hat for her husband back in Texas, we were on our way.

Dixie was awaiting the arrival of her friends, Pat and Bonnie from Wisconsin. When they arrived, we found that we all got along very well so Gil suggested we hop a trolley the next day and just ride it to the end.

The transit system in Quito is very efficient. The local blue busses charge 25 cents and like the trolley (also 25 cents) travel a north to south route. There are a zillion yellow cabs and usually for $1 - $2 USD, you can quickly get anywhere you want to go. Because we wanted to discover Quito, we opted for bus and trolley, only taking a cab when really necessary. Somehow, when you take a cab, you pay less attention to your surroundings and interact less. In a bus or trolley, you are in contact with the locals and because you don't know exactly what stop you need, you must use your Spanish to let the driver know. Most often, they remember your request and call out the stop. Never did we experience rudeness of any kind from a driver in Quito. (In Canada it is a 50-50 proposition.)

The next morning, we breakfasted at the hostel and set out with "The Ladies From Wisconsin". The streets in many cities in Ecuador and, I'm sure, in many other countries in South America, often bear the names of calendar months like, *10 de Agosto* or *Av 6 de Deciembre*. Two popular main streets are 'Avenue of the Americas' and *Amazones*.

The trolley was very busy but we all managed to get a seat. Bonnie sat across the aisle from me. She, like Dixie, had short, ash-blonde hair and a throaty voice. While we chatted, she took out her water bottle. Suddenly the cap blew off. It sounded like a gunshot. The trolley driver, in shocked confusion, stopped his vehicle in mid-traffic, while some of the passengers dove for cover. Someone called out, "*Que pasa*?" Embarrassed, Bonnie sat speechless but Gil and I called out in unison, *"Agua con gaz!"* While everyone laughed in relief, the driver restarted the trolley and we were off. Bonnie had bought a bottle of carbonated water (*agua con gaz*) and it had pitched around in her backpack. When she went to uncap it, it popped like a champagne bottle. It echoed so loudly, it sounded like a pistol going off. I am sure we jump-started everyone's day.

After that, we settled down to enjoy the view. Quito has a population of about 2 million. Apartments and homes ride up the high, green mountainside for miles and miles around but as we approached the outskirts, many barrios appeared and seemed to multiply like a cage of bunnies. Towards the end of the line, we saw a big mall in the distance and decided to visit it.

Like El Jardin, the mall was very modern but not as trendy. We split from the ladies and went off to explore the stores, compare prices (very similar to NA) and actually enjoy a 'real' coffee at a café. I went up to the highest level where tall, slanted windows gave onto the green vista of the hillside, making it a part of the malls' construct. I took some photos, then returned with Gil to join up with our friends in order to catch the trolley back to Old Town.

Eating in Quito is very cheap, especially if you have the *almuerzo* or lunch special. (In the evening it is the *merienda.*) The *almuerzo* often includes a delicious soup that must have simmered on the stove since early morning and usually consists of potatoes, carrots, corn, onions and a bit of *carne* (meat) or *pollo* (chicken). This is followed by a *segundo* or entrée, consisting of rice and/or *papas fritas* (fries), an *ensalada* (salad) of tomatoes, onions or avocado and a small piece of meat or chicken. The soup alone is very filling, a meal in itself. It usually costs about a whopping $1.50 U.S. We loved the *salsa picante*, which is similar to salsa in North America but made with purple onions – we pour it over our rice like gravy. Ketchup, or *salsa de tomate*, is very thin, so we passed on that. Vinegar is difficult to come by in restaurants. Often the special comes with *jugo* (juice), made naturally from pineapple, papaya or even watermelon. When you've had juice here, it is hard to tolerate what you get in North American stores. Natural is just not 'natural' back home.

Old Town Quito is much more spread out than Cuenca.

The cobbled streets ramble for miles and miles up and down hill. The sidewalks are very narrow and it is hard to avoid the native mothers below your feet, with their hands out begging for money, ostensibly to feed the child dozing on her back. Everything is 'out there' in Quito. The huge churches, the poor, the rampant tourists, stores selling cheap knicknacks and T-shirts, vegetable markets and vendors on the street selling their brand of tacky trinkets or snacks. Gil and I flew around taking pictures, taking in the energy and the sun shining down on our backs, as we ventured further away from the crowds.

We talked to a woman from Manchester who reported (perhaps facetiously), "There are no people left in Canada because they're all here in Quito". We looked high and low but were unable to find any pale faces with crazed looks from searching far and wide for Molson Canadian *cerveza*.

The next day, we took a bus to the infamous Otavalo street market, 30 or 40 miles north of Quito, with the Ladies from Wisconsin and enjoyed the bus ride through the mountains. We shopped the miles-long market all day and returned to our hostel with the sunset. I got to sit in the jump seat beside the driver with Gil beside me. While our bus passed another bus, a bus coming towards us passed a bus – on a two-lane highway! I didn't bat an eye. I felt as if

I observed this spectacle as if from afar, my body seated and calm, while my conscious mind watched and waited with emotionless detachment. Ho hum.

We met people from all over the world in our hostel. John and Magda live in Lithuania but he is Irish and she Polish. There was Werner from Switzerland, Johanna from Berlin, Larita and her beau from Alaska, and Kelsie from Manchester, who left us a fresh grapefruit along with a sweet note, when she left. Everyone has experienced the best and worst of South America. Everyone favours a different place. Some say Bolivia, some say Argentina and others say Ecuador. For us, the Peruvians are more polite and always say *'con permiso'* when they pass you on the street. Here in Ecuador, they briskly step by and if you fall off the sidewalk, too bad. Being Canadian, we'd probably jump up, brush off our pants, apologize for being in the way and even apologize for being in their country. We Canucks are too polite by far.

As for Gil and me, the stimulation of Quito provided a diversion from the problems that plagued us in Puerto Lopez. He kept to his promise to stop drinking and truth to tell, it felt strange not to see a mug of beer in his hand. Evenings we sat, up on the balcony fronting our room, reading books, sharing tea and sometimes preparing a simple meal in the communal kitchen. It was so convenient to be in a place where the Internet was right there, reliable and reasonable (about $1/hr.). We soon found out how convenient.

The small trailer park we owned in Nanaimo, sprung a leak. Well, not exactly. Sub-let tenants caused a rupture in the septic system from overuse and the very wet winter exacerbated the problem. The Health Department, the engineers and a septic system company were called in to pump out the excess sewage and water. Gil was on the phone constantly, on the Internet and sending faxes back and forth to find a solution to the problem. The money we were saving by our 'South America on a Shoestring' trip was spent rectifying the increasingly escalating problem. Finally, it was decided to put in a new two-step sewer system. After almost a week of this, I almost bought my partner a case of beer. Almost.

Through it all, we kept calm because there was so little we could do from so far away. Gil asked his engineer if he should return home and was told that "things were under control." However, we felt guilty, like two soldiers leaving a command post to sneak a cigarette during an enemy raid.

In the end, costs exceeded $40,000. Gil said, "This is the most expensive trip I have ever been on." Not just money, sometimes, but wear and tear on the soul.

Being with the 'Ladies from Wisconsin', though, I felt warm and safe, felt as if I was surrounded by three mothers, who were not only caring, but full of life and humour. My own mother back home lives in a care home for the mentally ill and, to my way of thinking, never really knew the joy of life, never truly experienced a rollicking, good time. Never knew a day without always feeling a little or a lot fearful. I didn't want to be like that. I needed a better paradigm for my future. What better ones than these fearless, well-traveled ladies?

THE LADIES FROM WISCONSIN
(On the right)
OTAVALO MARKET
NORTH OF QUITO, ECUADOR

A NUN FULL OF SOMETHING

Italy, in the eighteenth century. I look down and I am wearing a black cassock and the full white and black wimple of a nun. I am the oldest in my family and my mother was so proud when I took my vows. I have a younger sister and I know her to be one of my sisters in this life.

My son leads me back, back in time. By working together, we have both learned to regress each other to past lives. His episodes are very visual; he can describe the vein on a leaf, the taste of an apple in his mouth or the feel of the material covering his body. Being more of a kinesthetic person, I must rely upon my feelings, rather than the visual experience.

I am devout, I know this, but it is my duty to my mother and her pride that keeps me focused. However, the new priest is full of life and personality; I am drawn to him in a deep way. His eyes shine with humour and he possesses an affable charm that the other sisters and I cannot resist. I want to be around him all the time and he knows it.

On some weekends, I go to visit my family. My mother dances attendance upon me and my sister looks on in envy. The neighbors come by and ask for blessings. It is not my place to give them, but I give them just the same. I return 'home' to my sanctuary but it is no longer a sanctuary, because of the longings I feel for my man of God.

We meet in odd places and our hands brush each other going up or down the stone stairways. I seek confession with him, though what is it I have to confess? That I long for him, long for his touch, just another touch, and his brown eyes shining down upon mine? That I long to feel them on my body, have him remove piece by piece those bits of clothing that represent consecration to a higher being? How foolish. But the urges and yearnings never cease. I try to satisfy them in the night, but the guilt and shame plummet me into a pit of depression. Praying only helps me to climb out halfway.

Then, one night, my prayers are answered. We pass and touch. Suddenly, he pulls me into a dark corner, kisses me roughly and, pulling up my gown, plunges into my body. I am shocked but my need for him answers his. We meet like this and then I begin to sneak into his chamber late at night. I am often too tired to attend Vespers but I drag my spent body to the chapel and pray forgiveness and, the same time, search out his shining eyes.

I begin to make excuses not to go home to my family. Not just because of the troubling shame, but in case I miss a moment with my love.

At about the same time my gown begins to fill out, his eyes no longer seek mine. He has turned his attention to a lovely novice. My body cannot contain the anger and the hurt.

While another heart beats beneath my breast, I am forced to witness his burgeoning attraction for this foolish, stupid girl.

I make up an accusation against the girl. Whom do they believe? Someone with my status or this love-starved child? She is sent packing and the satisfaction is momentary, for he has continued to prowl and prey on others. I begin to realize it is his pattern and I am merely one of many. Like a musician, he requires many instruments for his repertoire.

I go home to face my family. My sister has married a local merchant and they are very well off, but she is unable to conceive a child. I study the disappointment in her face but then realize she is the answer to my prayers. My mother is angry but she quickly falls in with the plan, for she does not wish to lose status in the community.

The child is born at home – a boy. I immediately hand 'it' over to my sister. I don't want to study its face or its hands or, even worse, its eyes. She takes to the child immediately while I am relegated to the status of aunt. No longer am I my mother's pride. I have shamed the family by a secret that must never be spoken. My sister is possessive of the child, never allows him alone with me and I understand. I deserve the mantle of her, and my mother's, contempt.

I return to the church and learn that the priest has gone on to a higher calling. The charm that won me, won those in higher, more influential places. Because I have no other place to go, I stay in the church to teach others.

Years later, I learn that he is giving confessional at a church in Rome and I go there. Through the grille, I tell him what our passion has produced, that he has a child somewhere, who grows and thrives away from both of us. He, at first, is upset, but then he flings accusations at me. It cannot be his, who else had I submitted myself to? Then I know that where I have produced one, he has produced many. I leave as quickly as I came.

The bitterness stayed with me my whole life and grew, like another child, beating beneath my empty heart.

I know that the priest is Gil and the child, my youngest son. So far, two lifetimes that I have given him away by a secret pregnancy. In this life, he was more than wanted.

From the time I met Gil, he shared with me some piecemeal memories of his past lives. Often he said, "I was a priest but not a good one. As a matter of fact, I was a very naughty one." Now I believe him.

QUITTING QUITO

The 'Ladies from Wisconsin' left for Puerto Lopez. The night before, we gave Dixie, Pat and Bonnie some advice on where to stay, what to do (very little) and also emailed our friends, Kay and Dan, to let them know they were coming and to treat them like the great people they are. I think that if we had met them in Puerto Lopez, it would have been a lot more interesting place. As it was, I was going to miss them dearly.

When they went to pre-purchase their bus tickets, Pat later told us, both she and Bonnie received the senior's discount. However, they refused to believe that Dixie was the same age as her friends, though she showed them her passport and all pertinent information. Finally she went back behind the counter, lifted her hair to show the ticket agent some scars and exclaimed, "Surgico Plastico!" She got the discount.

This is what South Americans know of the North American way of life. Of course, they learn this from television and magazines. Movie stars change spouses like they change their underwear, faces suddenly appear younger, lips and cheeks frozen perpetually in place. To show global philanthropy, they adopt children from unknown countries no one can pronounce. Have lifestyles and homes that not even dreams can produce – in Technicolor, no less. Yet, for me, their world is foreign, as well.

As Canadians, we consider ourselves the 'poorer cousin' of the U.S. of A. Perhaps my fellow countrymen will debate this, but I rather enjoy the advantage of this perception. It allows me to be an observer, to be able to sit back and follow the antics of my southern neighbors and hopefully learn from their mistakes. Yet our cousins are fearless, never afraid of striking out, always the first to admit to their craziness and excesses. Even to that of their elected officials.

While we were there, Correa, the new *presidente* was inaugurated. The day before, we watched from our balcony as military helicopters flew all day around the Congress Building. Down in the street citizens held a protest against the outgoing president, which was odd, because the guy was gone, right? (Just trying to emulate their northern neighbors, I guess.) Everyone was out in full regalia and we wondered if Canada was present for the occasion. (Probably not, too busy watching the 'Vancouver Canucks' or 'Toronto Maple Leafs' on the tube.)

We took a bus to *Mitad del Mundo* (The Middle of the Earth – Equatorial Line) but were unable to access the museum as a couple thousand people and the military awaited the arrival of the new president, post-inauguration.

It was poor planning on our part so we took a bus back into the city to do a simple act of banking, which took up the better part of a day.

One bank would not allow us to take an advance on our Visas, so we were forced to take a long taxi ride to another bank, in the *Mariscal Sucré* district. We waited in a long line only to learn we had to access the bank machines on the outside of the building. I wished someone had inserted a computer chip under our skins before we left on this trip one that automatically activated to give specific, English instructions, when faced with this maze of complications.

Back in Puerto Lopez, a long snake-line to get into the only bank in town, was a daily sight. We once tried to wait but the line was so slow we gave up. Women were the main occupants of the line, as I guess the men considered this on par with housekeeping. They perched on the ground, on the cement ledges and gossiped with their neighbors. Mothers breast-fed their babies as they patiently waited their turn. I wondered if many really had any 'official' banking to do or was this their 'official' socializing day?

There were no bank machines in Puerto Lopez, so we were forced to take a bus to the outlying, larger cities to access them in the malls. On one outing, we had forgotten our passports and got away with using our B.C. Drivers Licenses to get a Visa advance. I am sure that the bank employee thought it was a new form of passport and our air of bravado must have taken us over the top. Inside, we were thinking, "Oh no, please, not another bumpy, hot bus ride back to town. Oh please, *Dio mio*."

The day before we left Quito, we strolled the streets of the *Mariscal Sucré* district and decided to go for lunch where the locals gather. One of the waiters drew us in and the special of the day was called *'Cerdo'*. He said it was a very popular dish and instead of looking up the menu word in our Spanish/English dictionary we decided, "What the heck, go for it."

When it arrived, it was cut into cubes and had the consistency of gelatin. We soon realized what we had ordered: pig skin. If Gil had been fluent enough, he could have told the waiter, we don't eat that stuff, but dry it and stretch it to make footballs. We pushed it around our plates, while the waiter hovered over us making kissing noises, as if to say, "What did I tell you? Delicious, no?" More the makings of a 'touchdown' than a lunch entrée.

Aside from that lunch, we were very sad to leave Quito but felt the time was right to move on. After consulting fellow travellers, our guidebook and map, we decided to head a few hours south to Baños, a resort town famous for its hot springs, scenery and gateway to the jungle.

Quito was so many things to me. It was the peace I felt with Gil not drinking. It was the stimulation of exchanging ideas with fellow citizens of this great Earth. Quito was a mother coddling and protecting a child fearful of venturing out into the world. Yet at the same time, it was that same mother saying, "Go ahead, go out and experience life but just remember, I am still here, waiting to take you back in…"

I thought of my family and how rootless we all felt growing up. I thought of my mother and how she had only known the cruel winds of change – usually through the machinations of an abusive, controlling man. Then I thought of the loss she experienced of the one man who loved her unconditionally – her father. I wanted to parcel Quito and send it to her so she could know that feeling again.

We took a long cab ride to the bus terminal, boarded our bus and after an hour or so, learned we had to transfer to another bus at yet another compound. There were only two more 'white' tourists besides us and when we arrived at our transfer point, we thought we were making a restaurant or bathroom stop, but this was not the case. We quickly boarded the next bus, which had seen better days. The driver kept a steady pace during the seemingly long bus ride.

Both Gil and I needed to use a bathroom desperately but the driver wanted to continue. After much arguing, he swerved into a gas station and gestured for us to make it quick. We got off and began running around like village idiots, searching for the bathroom, until we finally found it. No locks, no seats, no toilet paper. But, when you gotta go, you gotta go. Back on the bus, with a snort from the impatient driver, we were on our way.

EL MITAD DEL MUNDO - NEAR QUITO

MY MOTHER'S STORY

One day, I visited my mother at my sister's condo in White Rock. I was curious to learn about the death of her father when she was four years old, an event that scarred her soul for life. I took notes and went back home to write it down, as I thought it should be written. Later, when I showed it to my mother, she exclaimed, "Yes, that's how it was, that's how I felt!" For my mother's sake I want – and need – to tell it.

MY VERY FIRST DAY OF SCHOOL

I didn't start school until I was seven years old. I had to wait for my sister, who was a year younger than me, to be old enough so we could walk the three miles together.

We lived in a small Ukrainian community in Saskatchewan and so English was my second language. As in every small town, everyone knew what everybody else was thinking and doing. But that didn't matter to me, a seven-year-old, standing on tip-toes, anxiously awaiting her very first day of school.

The schoolhouse was everything you could imagine a schoolhouse would be. One-room, scarred desks, and in the middle of that one room, a huge, black, pot-bellied stove. It was imposing, of course. Why wouldn't it be, taking up so much space like a giant black beetle, with a gaping mouth constantly needing to be fed. But I didn't care. I was in the schoolhouse where I had prayed to be and it was my very first day of school.

When I was four years old, my father died. One moment he was there, all six-foot-one-inch of him, sweeping me up and back over his shoulders, so I could look at the world as from atop a high, happy mountain. And then he wasn't. I remember the funeral home, gazing at him lying still and silent in his casket. I remember touching his hands and hoping they would animate to sweep me up to dizzy heights again. I remember feeling betrayed and disappointed. I also remember sticking one finger up my nose and walking around in an endless circle. I don't think I was noticed for a long time, but finally a family member came over, removed the offending finger from my nostril and sent me on my way.

There was one thing I had noticed about my father as he was lying in his casket. His collar sat rather high on his neck. Not your ordinary collar. It was like it was custom-made for the occasion, and even though I was only four years old and dazed by death, I still wondered about that collar.

Now here I am, seven years old and it's my very first day of school. Finally, I would learn and while I was at it,

I would make a few friends in the process. There was so much to look forward to, don't you think?

It was the middle of winter. Instead of taking our recess in the bitter cold, we were allowed a little break, so we all converged around that big, black, pot-bellied stove.

Suddenly, I found myself in the middle of a large circle of children. My back was up against the stove and all these faces were staring, leering at me. Then they began to chant, in a monotonous rhythm, "We know how your dad died, we know how you dad died. He killed himself, he killed himself. Cut his neck with a razor. Cut his neck with a razor. Cut his neck with a razor!"

At first, I couldn't understand what they were trying to say, but gradually the horror of those words began to sink in. Suddenly it all came clear to me. My father, silent and still in his casket. That inordinately high collar he wore. The custom-made collar to cover a big scar. A razor scar. The terrible truth on my very first day of school.

All I could do, even with my knowing, was to shout at that cruel circle of children and call them liars. My father had been in a sanatorium for treatment of tuberculosis, and he had died there, a natural death. That's what my mother had told me, and so, of course, I believed her. But these children knew the truth better than my mother did, and here I was, seven years old, on my very first day of school, dying from the truth.

I don't remember how I got through that first, horrible day of school. Nor do I remember how I managed to get up the next morning, take my sister by the hand, and trudge those three miles back to that schoolhouse, to that pot-bellied stove to face those children again. And they were children. That was the thing. I was a child, too. But I don't think, ever in my life, would I inflict on another human being, the pain inflicted upon me my first day of school.

As I got older, I somehow learned the rest of the story, why my father took his life – took it away from me so sadly and cruelly. It seemed that my mother, being an outgoing and vivacious woman, had decided that she couldn't wait for her husband to recover from his illness. So she began to 'step out' with someone else. Her brother, a self-righteous, indignant man, took it upon himself to march up to that sanatorium, where my alive, but unwell father was trying to regain his strength. So this man, this uncle of mine, told my father that the person he loved most in the world was having it off with someone else. Then he left, content he had done his duty to all, to man and his community.

I don't know what anguish caused him to take that razor in his hands. Was it the first wave or the second? All I know is that the neck I loved to hold onto when I was atop his shoulders, was slashed apart by a razor-sharp coldness. I don't think I could ever imagine the blood, or how long it took before they found him there. My lively and loving father, so lifeless in his lonely, betrayed room.

Of course, I blamed my mother and I never stopped blaming her. I never attended another funeral in my life and whenever I saw a funeral procession, I would run and hide anywhere – anywhere, to get away from the thoughts that someone else's death dredged up. And thoughts of the grief of the one left behind.

I keep a picture of my father with me always. In it, he and his brother are out ice fishing and it looks like they have finished a good, hearty lunch. (Probably cooked by my mother.) They are leaning against each other, and my father's arms are folded up against his chest and there is a youthful, satisfied smile upon his lips and his eyes are smiling, too. I love that picture so much, because that is how I wish to remember him. Not cold and lifeless in a casket, with a too-high collar on his neck. But this way, as he was to me.

As for that leering circle of children, I never really got over that, either. I'm sure I must have made friends with some of them, somehow. Kids usually forget their cruelties or they go on to form another circle and fling some long-buried truth at some other innocent, ignorant child. I know I never became part of any circle in that schoolhouse. Nor did I ever become part of any larger circle as

I grew up and older, and went away from that close-knit rural community. The rural community that knew what everyone else was thinking and doing. Well, they never knew what I thought and did, I made sure of that. When you are seven years old, and it's your very first day of school, you learn – and you learn well.

LIZ IN BAÑOS

EMAIL FROM BAÑOS

January 10/07
Dear Family and Friends:
We have been staying in Baños for a few days at the Santa Cruz Hostel. We first moved into one building but it had no view of the lovely, green mountains all around us, so the manager, Roberto, suggested we stay in the other building next door. He moved us to the second floor and the view is lovely. It is only $6.50 U.S. per night a person here, cheaper than Quito, but seems to have another class of traveller.

Three French Canadians, one girl and two guys, are attractive and charming, but lacking in certain skills of, shall we say, consideration? Every day at Happy Hour, they sing the same song, over and over again, Ring of Fire, by Johnny Cash, and none have one iota of singing talent. Evenings, they cook extravagant meals in the communal kitchen but leave the icky remains for Gisela, the poor cleaning lady, to clean up when she arrives in the morning.

Playing dumb, Gil struck up a conversation with the trio and commented that some 'idiots' left the kitchen so dirty, how inconsiderate and don't you agree? I guess they got the hint because it's been a lot cleaner when Gisela arrives.

Yesterday had to be one of the highlights of our trip. We had met Holly from the States a few days before, a 27-year old engineer who had homestayed in Chile to teach English and is heading to Peru to work in an orphanage. The three of us booked a tour of the Pailon de Diablo, the Devil's Frying Pan (the famous falls here) and it was a three-hour trip in what is called a chiva, a truck with bench seats for carrying several passengers. It was scary, but exciting. We rode along the old Amazon Trail, right on the edge of the green mountain passes. We paid a dollar each to glide across the valley in an old gondola, then went to a bridge where, for ten bucks, you can swing down into the canyon on a bungee rope. (No, we didn't.) Then we continued on to the site of the falls. Gil's foot was sore, so Holly and I trekked down without him. We hiked down a kilometer trail of stone steps then a winding path leading to the lookout of the falls. Beautiful. Holly encouraged me across a suspension bridge. I say 'encouraged' as I am still working on my fear of heights. We met a couple, Reuben, a businessman from Quito and Maria from Texas, an aeronautical engineer. He was trying to convince her to come to live with him in Quito - the discussion is probably still ongoing.

The shared experience of only a few hours, the beauty, draws people together and those moments in time are embedded in one's soul. An Ecuadorian couple sat atop the truck with us and they were the only ones without digital cameras. They lingered down by the falls, took their time to enjoy each moment as we hungry tourists ran around taking photos to brag about and email to family and friends. How much we miss by observing rather than by experiencing.

I challenged myself many times on that short, beautiful trek and am very proud of overcoming the fears of riding in the chiva, as it seemed to skate on the edge of an abyss, fearing but daring to look down and breathing in the beauty of the offerings of this place. The return trip was especially wonderful as the driver played a Spanish music CD of mixed songs from South American singers. The voices matched the moment, the cool air, the sunshine, the green mountains and the company we kept.

It rains a lot in Baños, but if you can picture an Ecuadorian Whistler, with many restaurants, cafés, discos and hostels (instead of pricey hotels) and the green mountains above, surrounding the town like the sides of a bowl, then you have an idea. It is famous for the sulfur baths, which come from the mountains above and spas are everywhere. We have not availed ourselves of them but the almuerzos ($1.50) are to die for. We make our own breakfast in the small communal cocina, enjoy a big lunch in town and then have 'tea' in the evening. We have adopted Holly and she and my son, Rob, have begun an email correspondence.

Like with the "Ladies from Wisconsin" we formed connections that we would never have considered back home. Holly has become the daughter I never had and it will be heartbreaking to part from her. She will be leaving for Peru before us and I must force myself to keep from crying when that happens.

Our future travel plans include Riobamba, for the great train ride, then back to Cuenca, on to Vilcabamba, Loja and then across the border to Peru again. I cannot leave without a visit to Machu Picchu, my main reason for the trip. Will it be as magical as everyone says? Quien sabe? Who knows? Take care and you will hear from us again soon,

Love, Liz and Gil

CHIVA TO EL PAILON DE DIABLO

FIRST TIME ON EARTH

My son regressed me back to a time that amazed me. The year was 497 A.D. and I came to earth for the first time from another planet in the Pleiadian Solar System. I came in the form of a woman who emanated beauty and purity. Little did she know what was in store for her amongst the Earthlings.

I live in a cottage by myself and enjoy my time alone. The folk around me think it strange I didn't search out a partner, but that is not what I am here to do. I am a healer and distil herbs for poultices for cuts and wounds, for healing ailments on the inside of the body. I also heal with the energy emanating from my body and hands, but this does not sit well with the people, who keep a wary eye upon me.

The town has a council and each week, meetings are held to discuss issues, and solutions to problems. In truth, it is comprised of narrow-thinking humans, who have nothing better to do than gossip and ostracize those who are different. I know, since my arrival, discussions are rampant about where I come from and the suspicious nature of my abilities. Quotes from the Bible are a means of justification for condemning my actions, although they contend they arise from so-called altruistic intent.

I feel the energy around me grow dark, but I do not believe that any harm is intended towards me. I come from a place where there is no such word as 'evil' and thoughts are freely shared with each member of my society. I cannot read the thoughts of the 'dark ones'. When I try, I encounter a wall of resistance against me but I cannot stop my healing, because it is part of me and so many are in need of my gifts.

I am called to a meeting of the council. Separated from the rest, they call me to stand before them. In loud voices, they condemn me as a harlot and a heretic. I do not know what each of those words means. Some of my neighbors report they have seen me dance naked in the moonlight, but that has not happened and I am amused by their imaginative minds. Others stand, even those I have healed from dread disease, and they follow the rest, point fingers in my direction and cast me as a sorceress. I do not understand why they do this, when we have shared our hearts over many cups of herbal teas and they have been so kind to a stranger. Now it is like a tide turning against me.

The council takes a vote. While I stand with my head down, they condemn me to death.

Lying on the bed, my son tries to lead me to the last day of that life. My mind pitches and tosses like a boat on stormy seas. The memory is too painful; I refuse to allow him to lead me there. I say, "Please let me tell this from a distance." Saying a prayer of protection he encourages me to continue.

They boil me in oil! Even up until the day, I cannot believe the intent of these people. Oh God, the pain, the excruciating pain! How long it took me to leave my body. Looking down upon myself from above, I saw what was left of who I was. The body all melted, almost down to the bones and the blisters as large as wagon ruts. My hair floated in greasy strings and when asked to say a prayer of forgiveness to my killers, I could not. Finally, I give in and send a prayer to the ones who perpetrated this execrable hate upon an innocent creature. What satisfaction can one realize from all this? What was the learning purpose of this lifetime? Compassion is too small a word and my forgiveness even smaller.

Coming back, I knew who this group of people were, but cannot reveal it. I have experienced these people in many more lifetimes and they have little changed. I can forgive them now only because the boiled oil has become heated, slippery words of prejudice and judgment. Not as harmful, because I have often armed my psyche with detachment so they can no longer hurt me.

I should have returned to my home but stupidly remained on Earth to learn other lessons that still confuse me to this day.

Only One

There is one
Only one whose kiss
Will open these eyes
And pull back
This curtain of longing.
Lying alone,
        my life has been
Like a death,
        I need your breath
Upon my soul
        to give me life.
Do you know
How alone
I have been?
        Do you know
Even in sleep
        the pain
        seeps in?
But don't stop at a
Kiss...
Run your hands all over
The part of my soul
That is flesh.
You are the part of me
I lost before this sleep
Drew me in,
You are the part
Of me that
        time took,

Find me
Awaken me
Let's lose
          ourselves
Inside each other
Until time and flesh
Know no ending
No beginning
Twin souls
Awakening
We are
Only
One.

HOLLY

We left Baños after a week. I was sad to leave. This place, its peaceful energy, and Holly, too.

Our time with Holly was short, too short. She seemed to possess an aura of vulnerability yet, at the same time, she was fearless. Quitting her engineering job, she sold off everything and signed on to work in schools and orphanages, teaching English to the kids, while billeting in homes considered very basic, with people she'd never met, communicating in a language not her own. At her age, I had just given birth to my first son, was living a safe, secure life with a man with whom I'd promised to spend my life. Yet we were unable to communicate – even in the English language.

Gil and I met Holly our first day in Baños. We were having lunch in a restaurant and there was only one other person in the place. Like with meeting Dixie, we chatted back and forth, exchanging observations and information. She was from the States but had been living in Chile for several months and came to this town for a break, before heading to Huancayo, way up in the Peruvian Andes, to work at an orphanage. It was easy to joke with Holly, so we asked her to join us at our table. Later we learned she was staying at our hostel. The universe moves in mysterious ways…

I couldn't decide if I was to drawn to this young woman because she reminded me of me or did she unlock in me a need to have a daughter? You could only mother her so much because she had been on her own so long. Her dad had passed away when she was twelve and she and her mother shared more of a peer relationship, rather than the typical mother/daughter one. Yet I saw in her a need to belong somewhere, to be part of a larger family.

Holly fell into an easy rapport with Gil. They played games together, kibbitzed with each other and when the time came for conversation and sharing, that's where I came in.

She was in email contact with a male friend and they had made plans to meet up in Quito after her stint in Huancayo. They would explore this great city, travel to outlying areas and, from what I gathered, return home together. When she spoke of this man, her eyes glowed with hope of a possible united future. Yes, she was so much like me, still searching for a place to belong and a person to help her feel whole. For such an independent woman, she possessed a needy heart.

I admired Holly because she got her engineering degree, went to work, then realized it wasn't what she wanted. Not content to stick it out, she kicked it over for a South American adventure. What courage it must have taken; I know I could never have done this. For me there had to be a safety net.

While Holly stayed in our hostel, we naturally involved her in all of our activities. We lunched together, made supper at the hostel and enjoyed tea later in the evening. When we booked the chiva to take us to *El Pailon de Diablo*, of course she was a necessary and enjoyable inclusion. No one thought perhaps this was strange but then South America does that to people. Whoever you are supposed to meet, you meet. Time spent together is precious and without question.

You learn that places are what they are because of the people you meet. And sometimes, you meet yourself in a faraway place, or a younger what-could-have-been version of yourself. Holly was the latter, but sitting from my elder perch, I wondered if I could have been happy being her, making her choices. At Holly's age, I was the kind of person who preferred to opt out of making choices and if I made one, it was the one with the escape clause.

Though I felt motherly towards this young woman, the motherliness was tainted with envy. Sometimes we embrace what we need to face.

ON TO RIOBAMBA

We had read about the *Nariz del Diablo* (Devil's Nose) train ride in the Lonely Planet, so we made plans to head to Riobamba, approximately four hours south of Quito, to take the trip.

The night before we left Baños, the French Canadians at our hostel partied into the night. They hooked up with two girls who occupied the room next to ours. We smelled the 'weed' through the walls but that did not disturb us. Shadows raced back and forth across our window and loud, inane giggling kept us awake. Finally Gil pulled on his pants, marched next door and knocked – very, very loudly. Silence. I think they thought we were the *Policia*, because a few minutes later, soundless shadows tiptoed past our door, signalling the end of the party.

Gil assisted Roberto, the hostel manager, in making up a sign in English for the kitchen. He copied it out on the computer but didn't quite copy out the translation correctly. It read, "Please clean your dishes, and clean up after yourself. TANNK YOU." A little entertainment whilst cleaning the pots and pans. In the guest book we wrote, "We helped Gisela *limpia la cocina* (clean the kitchen). Our job is done here." We must move on to other hostels with a kitchen that needs our brand of psychological muscle. Mr. and Mrs. Clean of South America.

I did not like Riobamba. Our hostel was old, musty smelling. Suddenly we couldn't get along together anymore. It was as if the atmosphere of the whole place pulled our spirits down.

There was nothing I could see around us that would dispirit a traveller. Riobamba, as well as being famous for the train ride, was the place where the first constitution was written giving it the cachet of 'birthplace of the republic'. Beautiful Volcano Chimborazo towers high above the city at 6300 meters, making it Ecuador's highest mountain. They say all roads lead to this place because of the extensive infrastructure of highways from the coast, from the north, then south to the border. Being a bustling colonial city, it boasts the requisite Saturday markets, ubiquitous restaurants, plazas and Cathedrals. Yet I couldn't shake my feelings of melancholy. My kinesthetic nature folded up protectively, as if fearful of warding off some strange, psychic attack.

We bought tickets for the 'great train ride'. We were told to arrive at 6:30 in the morning, though we were not slated to board until after 7:30. Then we realized why. While standing in line for an hour, we were subjected to the continuous sale of hot drinks and snacks. Not just one or two hawkers, but many, many. Even a polite Canadian can get nasty at times.

Finally, we lined up to board. There is seating on the top of the train and many passengers are dressed warmly and place sheets of plastic over them to stave off the chill and possible rain. We climbed inside, where it was warm and comfortable. There were three trains, two like ours, which might be considered 'coach' because the third train was more upscale. A fellow passenger told us that this one costs a lot more, with plush seating and a meal served. Well, la-di-da.

It is a five-hour train ride round trip and the cost is about $14. U.S. per person. It goes as far as a village called Sibambe. It stops in Alausi, after about an hour or so, in order for passengers to search out a bathroom or buy the delicious *empanadas* the locals sell.

The switchbacks are scary, but the view down into the steep valley, with the flowing river and small houses perched desolately above, is very beautiful. Since I have already experienced close calls with my Maker on Andean roads, this was a cakewalk. Call me intrepid.

In Sibambe, the passengers on top can exchange seats with the inside passengers, but we decided to pass on that. Returning to Alausi, we opted to catch a bus back to Riobamba. It was a mistake. It was one of the longest two-hour bus rides on record and we regretted not staying on the train. Endless stops and the winding route made me nauseous.

I felt out of step and out of time in this place. It was a teeming city (pop. 126,000) , yet it possessed no personality. Its energy existed for this one main tourist attraction

It seemed when I was alone with Gil, without the protective stimulation of others, we were forced to face ourselves and each other. The fear of never being able to return home was always with me. In my first years with Gil, I used to have dreams of losing my purse containing all of my identification. It wasn't a stretch to reason I feared losing my identity in another relationship. These dreams arrived, full force, here in South America, yet it was my physical safety that was at stake, not my identity. But then again, I might have been wrong…

As for Gil, I found him to be increasingly controlling with our travel arrangements. Even the simplest task, like filling water bottles, had to be completed not later, but immediately. I began to wonder who was his peon last year? Not only that, what was he afraid of?

The day we left our hostel, we had a huge fight, which began with packing and organizing our suitcases. Somehow, we got in each other's way and before I knew it, Gil was heading out the door, threatening to leave me to my own devices. The argument escalated to a screaming match and at one point, Gil raised his hand, as if readying to strike me. We had both reached a breaking point.

"Go ahead, you want to do it. Hit me!"

"Don't tempt me!"

"Get out! I can take care of myself."

"All right, if that's what you want, I'm going."

"And leave me in this hell hole, are you crazy?"

"You told me to go."

"I've changed my mind."

"Well, what do you want me to do?"

"Stay, but stay the hell out of my way, until we get out of here."

"No problem."

MURAL – DOWNTOWN RIOBAMBA

RIDING ON THE EDGE

Many thoughts have been going through my head. It seems that travelling in South America causes one to ride on the edge.

There is the physical safety edge when you ride on a bus, high in the green, misty Andes and there is a rock face on the left and endless abyss below on the right. The bus driver passes another large vehicle on a steep turn, your heart jumps into your mouth and you feel as if, this is it, this is the end. The moment passes, followed by many more and after a while you think, well if I'm meant to die now, then so be it. On the edge.

Next is the edge of threats and personal safety. The fear of being robbed or having one's life threatened at the end of a knife or gun. Keep that bag close, don't let anyone touch your suitcases, be aware of your surroundings, don't go out in that area in the dark, they'd kill for your passport. Veiled threats at the border crossing, at Agua Verdes. In Baños, we watched a potential thief circling around us like a honeybee, pretending to watch the overhead T.V. in the bus terminal, but we knew better. You learn to use the antennae in the back and front of your head. On the edge.

Then there is the edge of pre-conceived concepts and beliefs. In Baños, we met Rania, a Palestinian whose parents started the first Israeli-Palestinian kibbutz. The Israeli government allegedly caused her relatives to disappear or be killed. The Israelis jailed her father for almost a year for participating in a protest seeking increased civil liberties. On his release, her family immigrated to Sweden. Rania knew so much loss and wanders continuously, working here, moving there, for fear of forming permanent emotional attachments. To think that the Jews could treat others this way after their treatment during World War II, boggles the mind. Our concept of a Palestinian was THEY were the terrorists, not the ones being terrorized. In South America, we learned to shift our thinking. The edge of perception and prejudice.

We thought that cities in South America were backward. In Quito, they have the most sophisticated transit system that would put many in North America to shame. And the fact that we expect rudeness from bus drivers as a matter of course, yet, here we were seldom treated with disrespect, only courtesy. As for technology, it seems that everyone owns a cell phone. Everywhere you look in cities, and even in a small village like Puerto Lopez, almost everyone has cell phones and many have computers.

We believe our technology and our extreme consumerism gives us the right to judge what happiness is. Observing the poor in Puerto Lopez, we think how sad, we have so much and they have so little. Yet, they have such a sense of family, extended family and community. Children are happy to play with a cheap soccer ball, or a dirty doll with one arm. Children are adored, cosseted and the whole family raises a child, not just the parent. However, as Raoul in Puerto Lopez explained, “Parents are totally unaware of the safety of their children. Children wander into the ocean, in front of cars or oncoming taxis. Then they say, ‘It is God’s will.’ The edge of expectation.

We have visited huge, Gothic cathedrals where the poor and crippled beg outside the ostentatious façade and we think, “All the money the Catholic religion spends and they can’t even provide for these poor.” But look at the East Side of Vancouver, where the poor sleep on dirty mattresses in alleyways and beg on the streets for money to buy their next meal. WE have a welfare system and it does not provide.

We think our medical system is far superior. We talked to a young, female doctor in Cuenca, and she told us new doctors are trained to be in tune with their patients. Interns are sent to outlying villages in the mountains and jungles for 3 to 6 months to learn about different diseases and their symptoms. They learn to help the very poor, learn what it is to pay attention to the whole person, learn about their family history. And if the doctor-patient relationship is not in sync, then another doctor is assigned to that person. In Canada, just as in the States, the doctor is merely a scientist with a stopwatch, who more easily writes a prescription for a drug, rather than actually 'listening' to what is really wrong with the patient, that perhaps all they need is a hug and a caring ear.

Dentistry is cheap and contrary to what many of us think, South American dentists are often trained in other countries, like the USA or Cuba, where they learn the very latest in cutting-edge technology. We think because we pay so much, what we receive is so much better. The edge of comparison.

Then there is the edge of your relationship with your fellow traveller. Gil and I have been 24-7 in each other's company. When we are tired and stressed, well, it can get pretty ugly. But when it is good, we are so in tune with each other, just a look and we know what is going on in each other's mind. We have had to jump, in a split second, out of the path of a speeding car, turn a quick corner when we sense we are in the wrong neighborhood, shared a look of joy when experiencing a sleeping Ecuadorian child, a waterfall on a mountain pass or gazed with rapture in a silent cathedral. There is no one I trust more than Gil and hope he feels the same with me. His sense of direction is so acute, I fear I rely on it too much to get us out of any situation. I am lucky to have someone with such an uncanny ability to maneuver through space so well.

We have learned we can go into any outlying village and be able to communicate, albeit in our version of Spanish, what we want, need or where we want to go or what we want to eat. We have learned a lot but still have so much more to learn. The past tenses of the language still elude us. ('We go here yesterday.') and sometimes our brains almost explode with the effort and frustration of trying to get ideas across. Riding on the edge of learning and communication.

Sometimes I get so homesick, I feel as if I am travelling on the edge of reason. Christmas was so hard for me because I missed my family, friends, and the familiar surroundings of the Island. And yet, how could I trade these experiences and how could my thoughts have arrived at these places, if not for this journey?

I guess the idea is being able to explore a new way of thinking. Exploring the inner and outer terrain of South America.

But sometimes NOT being on the edge would be a nice change.

LIFE AS A CEMETERY

One day, my sister and I went to the city cemetery. This was the year my marriage broke up. While we walked amongst the gravestones, I cried and poured out my grief, my anger and what led to my decision to leave the relationship. Our steps led us to the gravesite of her late husband.

He had died of bone cancer at the tender age of thirty-one. Here was a man who had lived two lives in one. Did he die because he had packed his life so tightly with so many experiences? Or did he know somehow he would die young so drove himself to cram many experiences into such a short life? But there was his gravestone anyway. Someone had planted alyssum and red begonias before his headstone, but the ground was hard and cracked. Somehow, my sister and I felt the need to perform some physical ritual so we both bent down and used our car keys to free up the soil for the struggling flowers. An elderly lady was tending the grave of her mother and she lent us her watering can. The ritual of replenishing what the earth gave up and what the earth took in, was completed. We felt somehow peaceful after that. Then we searched out our father's grave.

He had died in 1989. The only and last time we had stood before his gravesite was the day they lowered his casket into the ground. I remember it had to be re-raised because the gravediggers had dug the hole on the blank side of his gravestone. (That side was intended for my mother, but would never be used.) We were all very hungry, our bladders were full and we wanted to head back to the Greek Orthodox Church, where a memorial lunch was being served. My brother refused to come with us and we asked him why. He lit his cigarette and with a mock glint of determination in his eye, he replied, "I waited my whole goddamned life to see the old man six-feet under and I'm going to make goddamned sure he's going to stay six-feet under." We left him to witness his dream come true.

I had to admire my brother's honesty that day. He spoke aloud a truth we kept hidden in our minds and hearts. Yes, we felt relieved of the burden of his existence. His passing was not tumultuous or grief or guilt-ridden. It was merely the passing of a man who had long driven each one of us, systematically, out of his life. But my brother gave voice to what we secretly felt: We, too, were glad he was gone.

The strange thing was, here was the gravesite none of us had visited and it was so lovingly and carefully tended! Someone had planted red begonias before his headstone and on either side were two healthy, green nest spruces. The soil was pine-mulched and well watered. Our minds boggled. Who would have cared enough for this man to perform such an ongoing labour of love? Not his children, who seldom received any loving acts from him. Why would we water any illusions after his death? The mystery may remain but it would not preoccupy our minds for too long. We had all decided, on the day of our father's funeral, any conflict of thought or emotion would be buried along with him. My sister and I kept walking until we reached the road bordering the cemetery.

Before us stood the home my sister and her late husband had lived in, until his death. She'd sold that house very soon afterwards. The present occupants were playing with their young daughter out front. My sister made as if to pass by quickly and quietly, but I decided on impulse to call out and announce who she was. They were very welcoming and remembered her. They escorted us over the grounds and proudly showed all the changes that had taken place since my sister left. The father was a professional gardener and had landscaped the grounds with creativity and love. A lily pond was built right into the back yard decking and the perimeter curved with a sweep of lush plantings. As we walked and talked, I suddenly felt two small arms wrap round my legs. I looked down into the most beautiful set of loving brown eyes I had ever seen in my life. It was their young daughter and she looked to be about five or six years old. Long, dark hair tumbled down her tiny shoulders and as I bent down, she gave me a hug that tugged deeply on my soul. Her father teased her, "Why did you hug that lady? You don't even know her." She looked steadily up into his eyes and replied, "Because I visited her last night."

She spoke these words with such calmness, such strength, that we paused and gazed at her for one still moment. Her father asked, "What do you mean, honey? And she replied, "I can't tell you." Then she hugged me again.

We continued our rounds and it was then we discovered who the mystery gardener was, the person who had lovingly tended our father's gravesite.

Before his death, my father used to come visit his gravesite. (Perhaps he sought some sense of solace there or perhaps he went there out of a sense of the macabre, we didn't know.) On his way to his car, he would stop and chat with this family and sometimes they'd invite him to sit on the porch and share a drink with them. During one of their chats, he made a request. Would they be willing to tend his grave after he was gone? They would be glad to oblige such a wonderful, dear old man. So they did. Now the mystery was revealed to us. But there remained two more mysteries.

Mystery number one: Why was our father such a dear and wonderful man to others, but never to us, his dear and loving family? The family, who waited for but never received, his kindness and loving tendance. Mystery number two: Did the daughter of this family really visit me the night before in spirit? Did we share some form of soul connection? Or did she represent some form of message for me as I struggled through the final throes of my dying marriage? Well, let these two mysteries lie. Perhaps the solution of the one lies with the other.

I may not miss you, Dad, but I forgive you. And I may not miss my marriage when it finally ends, but I know I tended my hopeful illusions while sitting by its gravesite. My soul had not just cracked and dried during our marriage, but from the time of my childhood with my father.

Oh Dad, if you had just watered my spirit once or twice, I could have been in a different place and in a different time. Maybe living a real life. Not finishing, but beginning.

As we said our goodbyes, the little girl ran out to me again. I bent down and enfolded her in my arms and we kissed each other good-bye. I felt such an overwhelming feeling of love for her. It uplifted my heavy heart long after my sister and I left, long after I returned to my troubled life.

I know she will visit me again - someday. But this time I will know and remember.

VILCABAMBA

From Riobamba, we took a bus back to Cuenca and stayed in the Hostel Milan for a few days. It was a nicer experience than before, being situated right in the thick of the city. Our room was huge and had a great view of the Cathedral and the marketplace down below. We ate lunch there, then shopped for gifts to bring back to Canada. Consulting our Lonely Planet, we decided to hop a bus to Loja, the nearest city to Vilcabamba.

We learned that this village, high in the Andes, is known for the longevity of its inhabitants. If it's anything like Puerto Lopez, contemplation of one's navel is probably the most exciting activity of the day and who can't help but grow old gracefully?

I talked to Pedro on the small bus taking us to our destination. He is a transplanted Swiss and his real name is Peter. He's married to an Ecuadorian woman and was just returning from taking his five-year old to the dentist in Loja. We talked the whole time about food and especially salads, which are really hard to get in South America. Not your 'ensalada', which consists mainly of cabbage, but a real salad made of lettuce, ah lettuce.

My tummy ached hungrily for the taste of a Caesar Salad.

Then I mentioned to Pedro we had talked with Manon from France, with whom we had shared breakfast at our hostel in Cuenca. She told us, “I do not care for Vilcabamba. The ex-patriots there refuse to associate with the natives. Why go to a place to live and not be a part of the people, the life?” Pedro admitted that sadly, this was true. He was different because he had married into the people (he and his wife also had a two-year old.), saw the treatment of his adopted village by ‘outsiders’, yet felt powerless to change the dynamics.

Pedro got off the bus with his son and told us to look him up. How could we find him? “Just ask around for the family with the crazy monkey!” (They had adopted a monkey they found cruelly treated near Baños and now it was part of the family. Sounded like it ruled the family.) It is amazing how you can locate people here in South America…

Our first choice of hostel, the French-run *Hostal Rendez-vous* from the Lonely Planet, was full, so our taxi driver drove us down the road to *Las Ruinas de Quinara.* Farther away from the centre of the village, it was very lush with tropical plants and nestled in the curve of the green mountains. The owner, Mauricio, showed us around. There was a hot tub, pool and Ping-Pong tables. Our room was decorated in a feminine manner, with a white bedspread with pink trim and a mosquito net above the bed. (It rained a lot here and the combination of the humid days and cool nights, brought on the mosquitoes.) The view from our room extended past the grounds to the green valley and then the verdant mountains beyond.

The cost of the room ($17.USD) included three meals a day, so we decided to stay. Internet was free, as was the water. It felt like an ideal situation. The only drawback was the presence of a teacher's conference occupying the floor above us. The rules required that there be peace and quiet after 10 p.m. *"Todo bien,"* Mauricio assured us. All is well.

We met three strapping, blonde young men from Denmark. They were tall, handsome and spoke, not only good English, but also good Spanish, putting us to shame. They had taken six months off from their studies at the University and spent their time touring the States, Mexico, Cuba, Central and South America by bus. You could hear them joking back and forth amongst themselves in their native tongue – their energy light and gregarious. When the buffet was served for the regular meals, the female Ecuadorian servers smiled, preened, and added generous helpings to their plates. The same went for the teachers. When we held out our plates, it was instant snub and stinted helpings. We felt marginalized. When we came up for a second helping, they grimaced as if we were piggies. No matter how hard Gil tried to charm them with smiles and his brand of Spanish humour, they were not moved. *Todo bien.*

The next night, the teachers held a fiesta in the large room right above ours. We ran around looking for Mauricio, as the quiet hour had come and gone, but he was nowhere to be found. It seemed that every one of those teachers must have been wearing the same brand of steel-toed work boots, as the floor reverberated and pounded to their beat. We finally located our landlord and he smiled and asked, *"Todo bien?"* No, Mauricio, all is not well.

It quieted down for a while, then the disturbance began again. I went looking for Mauricio and found him sitting on a bench in the hallway. His t-shirt was wrapped around his neck and sweat was pouring from his face. He looked dejected but when he saw me, he weakly asked, *"Todo bien?"* I again asked him to see to the teachers and he shambled off to see what he could do.

I felt sorry for the guy. It seemed he was unable to please anyone and establish ground rules. The staff was all over the place, hard to pin down, and his wife looked to be a stern taskmaster. And now a mean Canuck was breathing down his neck. Couldn't get any worse than that…

We had planned to stay three nights, but after the 'fiesta of the teachers', the rains came. It rained all day Thursday, all night and into the morning. When we couldn't get hot water for our shower, when we got greasy eggs and grimaces for breakfast, when we couldn't find the rest of our laundry, we searched for Mauricio. All was not 'todo bien' in Mauricio's world. Time to get out of town.

It seemed that Gil and I drew closer because of our shared, jaundiced observations of Mauricio, our annoyance with the teachers and our treatment by the kitchen staff. Even with all this, it represented a humorous distraction and we laughed like kids on a camping trip. The focus was no longer on us anymore but upon our poor, set-upon innkeeper.

Something strange happened. Gil couldn't find his money clip with his American cash. We looked everywhere – in our room, in every pocket and in our luggage. Nowhere. He grabbed some extra cash, put that in his front pants' pocket and went to pay our bill. (Mauricio charged us $2. less a night.) We hailed a taxi and when we got to Loja, he paid the driver, then we went to the bus station to buy tickets to Piura, Peru. Gil reached into his pocket and all his cash had disappeared. Now he was out about $200. U.S. Grabbing some more cash from his body wallet, he went to get our tickets.

I stood by our luggage and closed my eyes to pray. "Angels and guides, if you are out there, please help us find our money." I prayed and waited for Gil.

Gil returned and then something made him reach into his body wallet. From it, he pulled out his money clip with all the money attached. He pulled out the cash he had supposedly lost from his front pants' pocket. It was all there. Every last dollar.

Todo bien.

***TODO BIEN*, GIL**

BURNED TO THE SOUL

Based on the following regression, I conducted some research on the Cathars. They were a religious sect, prevalent around the 11th, 12th and 13th centuries, mainly in France. The Roman Catholic Church launched a campaign to crush them, because they dared to embrace their own beliefs, one of them being reincarnation. The idea that control came from within, was an idea anathema to the Catholic ideology. This forced many groups to go underground, hiding in forests and mountain caves, constantly hunted and killed, sometimes in the most brutal manner.

I felt a thickening of my body. I intuitively knew I was a Cathar male.

I know my life and the life of my family are in constant peril. I am a father of two children, married to a good woman. We inhabit a small hut on a hillside and live off the land. I herd sheep, keep pigs and my wife grows what she can in the garden.

The believers meet in the woods and hold ceremonies there. We believe that our bodies die but not our souls. Life is hard and meant to be hard, but we've forged a tight community and that spiritual support keeps us fed just as the creatures feed and warm our bodies.

One day I came home from herding the sheep down the steep hillside. In the distance, I could see spirals of smoke and a sharp pain caught in my belly. I knew it was not the family fire; it was too thick and cloudy. I abandoned my sheep and ran the rest of the way dreading what I knew I would discover.

The house was burnt to the ground. I knew my family was unable to escape and I knew why. Pushing open the heavy, charred door, I saw their bodies hanging from the rafters. They looked inhuman, like bags of flour. The soldiers had come and not bothered to wait for me. What pleasure can they have gained from such cruelty? Did they not have wives and children of their own? These things I thought upon as I cut my children and wife down. These things I cried upon when I dug their graves and wrapped their bodies inside the earth.

I believed, like the others in my community, that the body is merely a casing and when life ends, life begins in another place. We go to a place of purification and our souls rest and play until the call comes to return to a new sheath. We are like swords put to the flames of drudgery, tempted by sin, yet tempered to a hardened brightness. Time and again we are tested for our loyalty and belief. My belief ended at the graves of my dear family.

I did not bother to rebuild our home. The sheep, goats and pigs wandered off for lack of care. The gardens faded and died. I roamed aimlessly in my grief, hunting and subsisting on what the forest offered. I hated those soldiers, hated the Church but also hated and blamed the community for my loss. I vowed to get even.

I knew the soldiers frequented the village inn. They invaded the place where we sought companionship. They taunted the villagers and drank themselves into stupors. The more they drank, the more maudlin they became. I went there often and also drank more than my fill. I listened to their talk, their threats and bragging of their foul deeds. Two in particular I watched, and knew in my soul they had participated in the killing of my family. Slowly, over time, they recognized me and sought out my company. To them I was merely a harmless dolt.

I played out bits of information, telling them I knew of the heretics, knew where they might be congregating. I told them what they believed – that they danced in frenzies to the moon, sinned with each other's wives, sacrificed lambs and their own children. They grew angry at my words, though they did not see their own actions as being sinful, but for the good of their religious creeds.

Finally I told them I would lead them to the community in the forest. They sent notice, an edict was given and more soldiers appeared. It was a long trek, but they forced me to march ahead of them, laughing at my back. I cursed them, cursed the people I once loved and cursed my life. I was Judas, selling my soul for a few pieces of silver. Had his feelings been destroyed, his beliefs cut into shreds like mine?

Is this how Judas justified himself? His soul empty, like mine –lifeless?

I lead them to the forest. You can hear the sounds of the community, everyone laughing and carrying on as if life goes on forever. Well, I know better. I stand back and watch as they whip their horses to a frenzy preparing for the great cleansing.

I stand back, punishing myself with the sounds of their horrified screams. They force everyone to build a cage. It takes the whole day, but I stand in place and listen and wait. They herd everyone into the cage – men, women and children. Then they set fire to it.

I convince myself they will be in a better place, like my family. I know that the smoke will overtake them, not the flames, but this is such cold comfort when I hear the moans, the coughing, choking and then, the horrific silence. I hear the soldiers' hysterical shouts of "Burn the heretics!" and the confused whinnies of the horses. Hell is not a place elsewhere; it is here and I created it.

I do not wait for the soldiers to return with my money. I run and keep running until my body aches with pain and sweat pours from every pore. I see the mountains and the steep cliff. Running faster, I feel triumphant laughter rise up from my belly, into my throat, and then I leap into nothingness.

I felt drained and exhausted with this regression. My consciousness railed against the idea that I, such a peaceful and caring person, could have betrayed people who mattered to me. But then what did I know of such grief and loss?

The question is sent out each time: what is to be learned from this? And always the answer is the same: compassion, love and forgiveness. Forgiveness for others, as well as for oneself.

In that lifetime, I reacted to the death of my family with feelings of revenge. Misplaced revenge but revenge all the same. I numbed myself instead of seeking solace from my community. I knew I could not deal with the fact I blamed myself for not being there for my family, though they would have killed me alongside them. I punished myself with my act of revenge, stayed to the bitter end and then ended my life.

But who would have welcomed me on the other side but my precious family? How ironic.

With each 'visit' to a past incarnation, it is important to send forgiveness to the ones who betrayed and hurt us. It is also important to ask for forgiveness in return. Why is that? Because it is a contract you make before you are born into each lifetime. A contract in order to learn soul lessons.

For me, the echoes from that life represented a form of self-punishment and what was written on my skin, was engraved in my soul. With each revelation, I learned to release the pain and self-abnegation. My skin did not improve overnight, but my acceptance, I noticed, reduced the redness. Like the redness of flames licking at my heart and soul.

Only the Beginning

Into this moment
 We call life
We pour our greatness
 Never knowing
That greatness flows
 From other moments
 Other lives

Discover in your heart
 Your greatness
Let it flow, let it know
 The source
There is but one
 The
 Infinite

The heart holds within,
 Your greater self
Live fully in
Your greatness
 Take hold
 Of that power
No one else decides
 You decide…
Listen to the voice
 That still, deep
 Quiet voice and then

You will
 Know -

 Believing is
 Only the beginning.

PIURA

Piura is two hours from the Peruvian border. We first bought tickets to Macara, which sits directly on the border (this one was not crooked or dangerous) but learned our bus was actually a direct bus to Piura, so we had to return to the ticket booth to upgrade. A couple from our hostel in Baños translated for us and not only were they taking the same bus, but the 'Danish contingent' from our hostel in Vilcabamba was heading to Peru, as well.

The ride through the mountains from Loja to Macara was enchanting, with a vista misty and green. We passed miles of rice fields and felt as if we could have been anywhere in the world - perhaps China or Japan - anywhere in time. I felt a sense of peace envelop me like a warm, cozy blanket. I wanted to keep going, keep riding our cocoon of a bus into tomorrow, into the next day and the next. The night closed upon us and we could no longer see the road.

The border crossing was easy but very slow. The Ecuadorian immigration official must have been learning 'Computer for Dummies' because he hunted and pecked on that thing until our brains were ready to fall out. It took an hour to process ten people. Then over to Peruvian immigration (our bus driver was a very patient man) but the official was nowhere to be found. We waited, (this time patiently as our brains, as I mentioned before, had already emptied). He finally arrived, got our forms filled out and then we were sent across the street for more questioning as to citizenship, profession and ages (painful for me) and then we were done.

We arrived in Piura about 10:30 at night, bade farewell to our travelling companions and booked into the Hostel Paracas (not in the Lonely Planet). We knew we would not be spending much time here, as the air was stifling and humid. In the daylight, we knew for sure we would not stay.

This city is very, very busy, with armies of moto-taxis, *collectivos* burping out passengers at every stop, motorcycles and taxis. Since it was Saturday, the streets teemed with people. I felt drained, so Gil went on his own to explore, while I remained in our air-conditioned room.

Piura's claim to fame is that it is the oldest colonial city in Peru, having been founded by Pisarro in 1532. (I am sure the humidity would have melted his armor in no time flat.)

There are many transplanted Chinese people here. I assumed they came here to work on the railroad in the last century and remained. It is strange to hear an Oriental speak perfect Spanish but after a while our astonishment faded into the woodwork. Besides, we were too busy enjoying the chop suey and chicken chow mein.

Gil complained incessantly about the price of food and I thought at first he was behaving like a cheap, grumpy old man. Then he realized we were now in Peru and the cost was 1/3 the price of the Ecuadorian dollar. He adjusted accordingly, by dividing the cost on the menu by 3 (3 Soles to the dollar).

PIURA

Our room was in an older hostel, but close to stores and restaurants. The walls were lined with mirrors and I wondered if the owners thought a typical traveller from another continent would prefer this type of décor. Kinky night for the old folks.

When Gil and I got together almost twelve years ago, we couldn't keep our hands off each other. We made love on every available horizontal surface. Relatives told my sons that Gil and I had gotten together 'just for the sex' not considering to take into account our thoughts and emotions. However, had we continued to mindlessly sate our bodies, perhaps we never would have experienced all the issues we did.

I once told Gil, "You control with sex, did you know that?" He made it clear to me from the outset that it was a very important component of his life, which was a way of saying, "I need it, when I need it, so you'd better be available." If we weren't fighting about money, then it was a push-and-pull about sex.

During the course of our relationship, I experienced the onset of menopause and whether it was psychological or not, the libido slowly slowed to a simmer. I suggested to Gil that he read up on this stage of a woman's life, in order to understand the changes, how it affected us as a couple. He 'Googled' it and read up on it a bit but not enough for the information to sink in, because the script lines of, "You used to want it a lot when we first got together," never really changed. But ***I*** changed.

LIFE AS A BEACH

There is a little beach down on Lake Ontario that is today, little known and little used. Little used because there is a waste treatment plant situated adjacent to it and the emanating smells would knock the breath out of a skunk, let alone a potential picnicker or sun bather. Little-known because there are no signs leading the way to it, so the only people acquainted with this little beach are the near-by inhabitants or anyone who might accidentally stumble upon it.

I know about it because I lived down by that beach when I was a child. Those days down by the beach, Municipal Beach, are the only almost-happy days I can remember from my childhood. But they were short-lived. My father saw to that. Our family lived in an almost-two-storied house just up the hill from the beach. I say 'almost' two-storied because my dad started it, but never finished it. He never really finished it because it burnt down. And that was the end of my almost-happy childhood.

The happy things I remember, let me see. The french fries. There was a man called Sam who worked the re-freshment stand at that beach in the summer. Back then, people came here to picnic, swim in the (we thought) un-polluted waters. Those french fries were the best I ever tasted in my life. They were sold in paper cones, and I loved to soak mine in so much vinegar, I thought my cone would sog up and collapse. It didn't happen because I devoured those french fries so fast, the vinegar didn't have time to soak through the paper.

Sometimes, if it was a slow, overcast day or it was getting on towards the end of the season, Sam would offer up his fries for free. I think they were about fifteen cents back then, but back then fifteen cents went a long way. The idea of free fries and still having money in your pocket to run to the corner store and satisfy some other major craving, was a mighty thrill for a kid in those days. It is a feeling I can summon up even now. I think it's because Sam knew many of us kids were poor and barely able to afford any extras that he offered free samples. It is his generosity that stays in my memory, I am sure.

The canal was on the other side of a small stretch of woodland near our beach. In those woods someone had hooked up a long Tarzan swing over a pond. If we weren't swimming in the lake, we were all down by the Tarzan swing. I was too young and too scared to take my turn, but I loved to watch the other kids as they whooped, screamed and flung themselves over the pond, letting go of the rope. I have dreams sometimes of standing on the little hill overlooking that pond. I grab onto the rope and just as I am swinging over the middle point of the pond, I let go. But I do not splash down into the water. Instead I am flying over and then far away from it, towards the mountains and even farther away, towards the stars.

My cousins came to visit us from their farm one or two hours away from us. We camped in our covered porch and told scary stories by flashlight. The one about the mass murderer with the hook instead of a hand had to be the scariest. Just as he was going to kill a couple kissing in their car down by the canal, they saw his shadow in the rear view mirror and raced away. When they got home, they found the hook stuck in the car door. The storyteller, usually my brother, would suddenly turn off the flashlight, leaving us screaming, scrambling and trembling in the dark.

Sometimes a night rain fell and I loved the sound of the drops plip-plopping on the tin roof. Nothing can hold a candle to that memory, to that sound. And speaking of candles, that is how my father burned our house down.

It was the end of summer and my father decided to take us to visit our various aunts and uncles. The car was packed and off we went.

People remember what they were doing and where they were when John F. Kennedy was shot in Dallas. I remember where I was and what I was doing when we heard our house had burned. Down by the creek, behind my aunt's house in Simcoe, scooping up polliwogs into a little tin pail.

A neighbor had called and told my parents. They surmised it was a gang of vandals who had broken into our home, drank beer, and played with matches. There were empty beer bottles strewn inside the covered porch as evidence. Why couldn't they have just vandalized the place, but left our house still standing? What cruel, cruel creatures.

My brother was the bearer of bad news. We stood together and cried, our pail of polliwogs abandoned at our feet. To this day I can never think of those sperm-like things that became frogs without the image of that house, our home, charred and burnt and the feeling of homelessness and hopelessness.

I didn't find out until years later from my eldest sister that it was my father who had set fire to our house. He had set a lighted candle on a wooden chest and while it slowly burnt down, we headed out ignorantly and happily on our family vacation. With a mind like a criminal, he thought to set out empty beer bottles to make it look as if some delinquents had broken in, drank a little too much and decided, in their cruel inebriation, to torch the place. How proud he must have been, fooling the insurance people, fooling his own family. Dad's brilliant, malicious touch.

My sister knew because my father tried to bribe her to set up the scene. She refused and then forced the memory of his vile and selfish act to the back of her mind until we were older and could handle the truth. Perhaps she wanted us to hold onto just one illusion for a few years longer...

We moved into a two-bedroom house in the east end of our city. It was literally 'on the other side of the tracks'. That was all my father could afford, because the house near the beach did not burn all the way down and the insurance only paid a partial benefit. His bitterness, as a result of this poetic justice, seeped in and corroded what little was left of our sense of family.

After I learned the truth, I felt an almost-sense of relief. The years after we left Municipal Beach were depressing, unhappy years. The line of demarcation between the time before and the time after our house burnt, was firm and strong. These were happy days; those were unhappy days. Somehow the knowledge of my father's foul deed erased that line and smoothed everything over into one unbroken whole. If those happy days were an illusion, then so were the miserable days after. I felt safe and protected in that thought.

VERY TIRED

It was the end of January and I felt tired of travelling, tired of taking buses and staying in endless hostels, felt tired overall and wanted to go home. I sent an email to my family and friends.

Dear All:
Sometimes one gets very tired of travelling because, after a while, things just keep repeating themselves. Here are a few things I find very tiring:
I am tired of being the only white face for miles around, tired of the natives looking at me as if I was one of those cute, trained monkeys. Oh look, one of those white folks, let's see what stupid thing they are going to do and say next...
I am tired of visiting another colonial city, with colonial buildings and a big square with a big statue on it, and the name, "Plaza de las Armas". Have an original thought, name your square something like "Plaza de Las Arms and Legs". So you have a history, get over it...
I am tired of going to bathrooms in bus stations and restaurants that have no toilet seats, no toilet paper and no soap to wash my hands. I got smart, keep a roll handy in my bag, but am tired of being that smart...
I am tired of showers that trickle down to nothing in the middle of a good lather, tired of showers that are tepid, tired of primitive bath towels, tired of tiny little soaps that last only one wash. I am tempted, when the water runs out, to tramp naked and soapy to the reception desk so they can get a good look at what a disgruntled, cranky North American traveller looks like 'agua-interruptus'...
I am tired of naked light bulbs in hostels. Most of the time you can't even read under them, they are so dim. Makes me wonder if they

assume we are white travellers who never read. Just one of those albino monkeys...
I am tired of trying to learn this language and feel like I am getting nowhere, pronto, like a gerbil on a treadmill. Just give me a pill, I'll take two and call you 'amigo' in the morning...
I am tired of Gil's endless, nauseating enthusiasm about travelling. If he tells me how much better I am, what a good, little traveller I am, I am going to strangle him with his money belt...
I am tired of dodging yellow taxis, moto-taxis, busses and any other vehicle with wheels and a motor. I am tired of grabbing onto Gil's hands, taking a deep breath and putting my life on the line. These people may consider us target practice. What's another dead, Norte Americano turista anyway?
I am tired of meeting other white faces and being the first to say, "Hi, where are you from?" Really, I don't care, you probably don't care, let's just ignore each other and pretend we aren't the only pale faces for two hundred miles around...
I am tired of being tired. Maybe you would like me to pretend this journey is one big high, but it isn't. Tomorrow I may feel differently, but right now, this very moment, I would like to close my eyes, tap my red heels together and be whisked off to Kansas. O wait, no, that's Dorothy and Toto in Oz. And this is Liz and Gil in South America. Oh, give me a home, where nobody roams and I will be happy all day...
Okay, tomorrow is Tuesday, then that means Chimbote, Huaraz or Lima or... let's call the whole thing off. Will write soon from the next oldest South American city in the world.

Love Liz and Gil

TOTEMS

Sitting high upon the totem
Spirits entertain creation
Calling, conjuring
Ageless, timeless visions
Wooden is my command
Though my spirit
Is air and the wind
Whirls and soars
On currents of eternity

Totems are symbols
We grasp them
In the talons of our mind
Shape them through time
Taking hold
What was once
Myth and Mystery
Now fact
The vision no longer
The totem left behind

On the spiritless current
We kill creation
By seeking
To define

MY WARRIOR SOULMATE

I am standing in a clearing in the forest. I feel I am living in what is now called the Appalachia in the Northwest United States in the 16th century. I am a female aboriginal and married to a man who does not appreciate or love me.

I look at my reflection in the lake and see a young Indian woman dressed in deerskin, wearing pull-on moccasins, almost like boots. My cheeks are plump and I have a pleasing face but not pleasing enough for my mate.

One day, I am walking in the forest and I see him. He is from another tribe, but not a warring tribe. I see his skin, taut and glistening, in the light through the trees. He is focused upon a small creature, his bow and arrow readied to kill. He hears my footfalls, though I try to be quiet, but too late. I see the anger in his eyes and then I see something else. Recognition.

I know our spirits had joined in our sleep. My sleep was always restless and unhappy, unfulfilled. When I finally dreamed, I dreamed of a man of strength and love.

We stood upon the forest path and knew each other. Feeling afraid, I ran away.

But I saw him again. When I had done my duties with the other women and for my man, I took out the canoe and paddled the river from end to end until the twilight dimmed my sight and I was forced to return to the place of my unhappiness. But then I see him, coming towards me in his own canoe. His strokes are powerful and it is not long before he is beside my craft. We study each other's faces, eyes, hands and bodies. I am shy because my husband teases my shape, calls me a plump pear. But his eyes see only my heart.

Knowing who he is causes my life to grow worse. My husband senses a change and makes my life more difficult, filled with more tasks to keep me always busy and chained to the camp. But now, I have a reason to work faster and escape. I always know where to find him.

He teaches me about hunting, about spoors and tracks of animals, how to hold a bow and arrow. He wishes me to learn to be strong and self-sufficient. He doesn't care that women are not allowed to touch the weapons of our men. Doesn't care that this would contaminate them and cause the hunt to fail. I am a good student and under his tutelage, I learn well. I also learn to love him more than in my dreams.

Time goes on, the seasons circle by. Sometimes I don't see him for one full cycle of the moon and yet I do not despair. We still meet and love in my dreams; his strength comforts me and keeps me warmer than the bearskin in our marriage tent.

My husband grows discontent because I cannot produce a son. My body, I know, waits for another's spirit to grow inside.

I cannot take this any longer. I gather what I can and run away from the tribe. He is easy to find because my heart always knows where he is. We take our canoes and side by side, search out a place to start a new life together. By leaving our tribes we both know the consequences if we are found.

How can I describe the days of freedom we shared? There are no words.

One day, we are hunting in the forest. I am as good a hunter as he. I follow the trail of a white-tailed rabbit and determine to make my kill for our evening meal. Suddenly I feel a great pain in my side. An arrow passes through, striking vital organs.

I scream and fall to the ground. Quickly, he is at my side and sees immediately what he must do. When he removes the arrow, I pass out from the horrible pain. The next thing I know, I am looking up into his dear face. He is kneeling by my wounded side and smearing a poultice of herbs from a wooden bowl. I caress his face and we both know I am going to die. I promise him I will see him in his sleep. Our spirits will be together there, until he joins me when the Great Spirit comes for him. The pain is so bad, and then there is no pain at all.

I do not leave him, although we cannot touch. I walk beside him in his aloneness. I know that it was my mate who hunted us and then punished me with his arrow. For nine years my love wanders, then cold revenge is taken upon him, as well.

I see my old mate dig the hole in his canoe. I see my love get in, though I cannot warn him. When he plies through the rapids, the water floods into his craft. His canoe overturns and then my spirit eyes see his body floating in the stream down below between two rocks, like a sorrowed, drowned bird.

We are joined together now. We still hunt and he teaches me the best places to find succulent berries, how to know each trace of each creature. Nothing has changed except my wound is no more.

PERCEPTIONS & COMPARISONS

The Peruvians and Ecuadorians we talked with perceive Canadians as French-speaking Eskimos. Sadly, a lot of Americans have that concept of us, too, though they live a lot closer.

We talked to taxi drivers, people on the bus, storekeepers, restaurateurs, and hostel managers and the general consensus was that Canadians are friendly, speak funny, are more reserved and more polite than the Americans. As when we visited Europe, (and Greece particularly), we were treated rudely when they assumed we were Americans. As soon as people learned we were Canadians, their attitude shifted.

South Americans approached us openly and asked many questions. *What is the weather like now where you live?* Wet, cold and rainy. *Does everyone speak French?* No, but there is a province that mainly speaks French-Canadian. Most Canadians only speak English although there are many with a French heritage. *Is this your summertime?* No, we are experiencing our version of a winter on the Island. However, in other parts of Canada, it is very cold in the winter, a few meters of snow. *Is your summer very hot?* Our summers are cooler on the West Coast of Canada but the weather patterns are changing. We used to enjoy mainly sunny, dry days but the last few summers have been cooler and wetter. (Summers are more humid and sunnier in other parts of Canada). A bummer for planning weddings and picnics. Okay for threats of forest fires.

In Huanchaco, we met a contingent of Peace Corps workers and were amazed at these young Americans' lack of knowledge of their own country. One girl openly admitted she had no idea where Ohio was (to be honest I cannot really picture it on a map, but I am not a product of the Land of the Free and the Home of the Brave.) They even exhibited a marked lack of knowledge about Canada and seemed to be on par with the South Americans in their perceptions. The Europeans, on the other hand, were up on world events, geography, history – putting us all to shame with their savvy.

We encountered few older Americans on our journeys, as many in our age group opted to take the safer tours, stay at pricier hotels. We met a few in the hostels but they were younger, more adventurous and travelled on a limited budget. The Ladies from Wisconsin were an exception.

In Puerto Lopez, we talked with a tour boat operator who was trying to sell us tickets to visit *Isla de la Plata* to see 'blue-footed boobies'. (I'm not kidding. It's an indigenous bird that is actually has blue feet and is goofy looking.) We declined but he hung around and, with our careful Spanish, we answered his questions. We mainly compared our cost of living with an average Ecuadorian. We told him how much a car costs, housing, taxes, income and how it is multiplied several times by selfsame aspects of their way of life. The guy was blown away with how much a Canadian must pay to survive and through his perception, we realized what a heavy a burden we shoulder with so many taxes. Though the average South American must scrape to make a living, their expenses can be quite minimal. (For example, a motorcycle costs between $600. - $700. U.S., while we pay three times that in Canada. Wine is very cheap at about $2. - $2.50 a liter and *cerveza* approximately $1. U.S. for a large bottle.)

The tour boat operator expressed bitterness that the local government refused to infuse the village with funds, to help improve infrastructures to make it more attractive. The guides were the ones on the front lines selling and ferrying the tourists to various locales with so very little to show for it. We nodded, as we cast our gaze upon the giant tree roots blasting through the sidewalks. They will probably never know repairs until the government changes its attitude, or until land developers 'discover' this little gem and then change-purses will open.

No matter how poor a South American, they can still subsist on what is available on the land and in the sea. Fishing is still a very viable living and costs for a cod-like fish called *corvina* depends upon which vendor you are dealing with. Mainly it is $1.25 US. per pound (already filleted) but they offer cheaper prices to each other - a different 'kettle of fish'. Fruit, like limes and lemons, you can pluck from the nearest tree and vegetables – you can buy a shopping bag full for $1. U.S. In North America, to be poor is to be hopeless and helpless, less dignified, regardless of our so-called safety net.

Many of the homes in Puerto Lopez have dirt floors, but many citizens own televisions and cell phones. We learned that Internet arrived only two years before and the cell phone just before that. The cost of electronics and appliances is almost comparable to what we pay in Canada, so we wondered, "How do they afford this?" Perhaps they save for years or, like many of us, purchase their needs on a time payment plan.

Medical and dental is very reasonable in both Peru and Ecuador. Many medications we can only access through expensive prescriptions in Canada, you can buy across the counter here. *Farmacia* personnel are very knowledgeable about ailments and dispense medication with the expertise of medical doctors. After my experience with altitude sickness, I did not hesitate to trust their savvy.

We are considered very wealthy to the Peruvians and Ecuadorians. Many times, we modest Canucks rush to correct this perception. We are middle-class and proud of it. Well, no, we just don't want to be robbed and land up in a ditch, a dead, perceived-as-filthy-rich, gringo. (If you travel to any Latin American country please leave your Rolexes and gold and silver jewelry at home. Aside from the silver ring we bought in Chordaleg, Ecuador and the watch Gil bought off a street vendor in Quito, that was the extent of our show of affluence.)

What we found interesting was how many non-smokers there were in both countries. In Lima, we saw more smokers but in Ecuador's large cities there were comparably less. We thought perhaps it was the cost factor but in Nicaragua there were a lot of smokers amongst the poor. We learned that the tobacco companies gave out free cigarettes to get their target consumers - the young – addicted, then raised prices accordingly. In both Ecuador and Peru, we observed no evidence of this.

Except for our fearful brush with graft in Agua Verdes, Peru, we found most South Americans to be open, friendly, kind, curious and helpful. They were reserved (except for the open-air baby nursing.) and modest. Unlike the Mexicans, they were not resentful and dependent upon North American dollars. They managed to do very well without our filthy lucre, although it is the Europeans who seem to be the smart ones investing in these countries.

I really appreciated how dignified these people are and sometimes how over-the-top generous.

In Quito, we met a lovely lady who was the proprietor of an ice-cream shop. We had stopped to tour the gorgeous cathedral nearby and she was taking a break with her granddaughter, leaving her shop unattended. We talked and when we told her where we were from, she said she had family in Toronto. Both Gil and I hailed from Ontario so we shared information, then moved from that topic to Machu Picchu. She described the wonderful energy there and I expressed my wish to visit this magical place. She insisted we come to her store and have a free ice cream. We wanted to pay but she insisted we were her guests. She was so happy to share with us; we could not insult her by refusing her generosity. With hugs all around, we left.

The children were the most fascinated by our pale faces. Everywhere we traveled, they gathered around us, to touch us and listen to our mangled attempt at communication. On a bus in Quito, a mother and son teased us about our pronunciation and throughout the ride, taught us how to enunciate and gave us a few pointers on slang expressions. The son was reserved, at first but after realizing we were not scary and fierce, joined in the fun. I hope this gave him a new appreciation of ignorant *turistas* after that.

We got the impression that the aboriginal people or indios were treated as second-class citizens. There seemed to be a lot in the cities, perhaps because they were displaced from their land and forced to beg on the streets. They were shrugged aside by the citizens and some were even pushed or ignored. Yet many shopkeepers provided coin and free food when they stepped inside with their hands out. They represented the old ways, I suppose, and perhaps the 'new' South American did not wish to be reminded of their humble beginnings. (The sight of an Ecuadorian elder using a wall as her personal potty, is an example.)

When we attempted to take pictures of indigenous people at markets or in their villages, we learned to ask first. We assumed that perhaps they were superstitious and thought we would be 'stealing' their souls and locking them in our cameras. However, it is more a sign of respect. Often, it was a matter of a few coins in their palms, which brought welcoming, toothy smiles and 'here, hold my baby'.

We traveled mainly by bus and our preconception of sitting neck and neck with a load of chickens was not far off the mark. There was one local travelling with a chicken in a hemp sack. No goats or pigs were allowed, thank God. (They probably would have taken the best seats.) The elderly were never left standing and there was always a young person who immediately jumped up to give up his or her seat. I noticed, however, that passengers were less inclined to give up their seats to the indigenous elderly and this bothered me considerably. I offered my seat a few times and was refused with a curt shake of the head. After a while, I stopped and accepted this state of affairs as the way things are.

We constantly had to assure friends and family that South America was not a scary place to visit. Their perception was of gangs of *banditos* hiding in banana trees waiting to drop down on the heads of innocent, stupid travelers. After slashing our throats, having their way with me, and scalping Gil… (no, that's The Last of the Mohicans…) they'd disappear forever with our money, clothes and passports, leaving us bereft and without means of a return trip to our homeland.

There are certain areas you would not venture into in Vancouver at night, like the East End. Similarly, you learn from other travellers not to walk in some parts of Quito, take a taxi everywhere after the sun sets. In Puerto Lopez, we walked everywhere, anytime of day or night. In Cuenca, we were a little wary but there was always army or police presence wherever you looked. There was usually more than one, armed guard at a bank and, at first, this was a little daunting. But they treated us with respect and friendliness, so we grew accustomed to those scary rifles under their arms.

Because of our bad experience at the Peruvian-Ecuadorian border, we warned fellow travellers to go through Macara instead of Agua Verdes. It is even better to take a bus straight across so you can get processed in a safe group. This was hindsight for Gil and me, but our troubling encounter with crooked police and equally crooked 'guides' set an initial poor impression, which worried dear ones back home in Canada. And who can blame them? If one of my sons was travelling to a strange country and wrote an email about this same experience, I would have wired him a first-class ticket home, pronto. No matter how much we tried to still their qualms, we could not convince those waiting behind that many places we visited were safe, if not safer, than where we hailed from. Their preconceptions, like ours before we set out, were set in concrete.

And so, the filthy rich, ever-intrepid, French-speaking-Canadian-Eskimos with pale faces and forked tongues, journeyed onwards to their next exciting South American destination

HUARAZ

Email to Family and Friends
February 2/07

Dear All:
We are in Huaraz, situated high in the Andes Cordillera Blanca, with an elevation of over 3,000 meters (10,000 feet). We left Trujillo at 9 a.m. and arrived in Chimbote, where we changed buses in the afternoon. We did not realize, when we left the bus station, what a wild ride we'd be embarking upon.

If you can imagine something out of Indiana Jones' "Last Crusade", you've got a good idea. We rode in a small bus with our luggage strapped on top. Little did we know that, after just a half-hour of paved roads, we'd be traversing up, up on single-laned, gravel roads seemingly carved into the granite face of the mountains with the raging rapids of the Rio Santo below. Sometimes, it seemed as if the bus hung suspended in mid-air as it roared over narrow divides and then through tunnels carved into the mountainside. We rode through narrow canyons with rock faces shooting straight up like spires on an enormous cathedral. In my whole life, I have never experienced such a breath-taking, heart-stopping ride. I went from "very tired" to "scared but very alive" in the space of a few hours.

After 7 hours of continuous driving, we reached our destination of Huaraz (population 80,000). The place was almost destroyed in an earthquake in 1970 and yet, they are only just rebuilding the main plaza. Yungay, a town we passed on the way, fared worse, as almost all of the population of 18,000 were buried beneath the rubble in that same earthquake.

Huaraz is also situated on a major trail from the coast to the Amazon pre- and during Inca times, up to the Spanish invasion, 500 years ago.

We came here to visit the Ruins of Chavin de Huantar, located about 3 hours away from Huaraz. Built around 1200 BC, the complex holds ceremonial rooms and pyramid structures made of massive stone blocks. There are underground galleries and inside one, is a 15-foot obelisk carved in white stone, featuring felines, birds and snakes.

Our tour guide, Hugo, spoke only Spanish and you could tell he loved to hear his own voice. He began his seemingly endless spiel at the beginning of the bus trip and even those who could understand, grew glassy-eyed after a while. When we arrived at the ruins, Gil and I drifted off and explored on our own. Luckily, we ran into another tour with a guide who spoke passable English. He took the time to explain that the number 7 figured mystically in this Incan society – everything from stairways, to their art, to their pagan worship. Once the number 8 was reached then the process of life and death, fertility etc. began anew.

Yes indeed, we have our virgin sacrifices, bloodletting, you name your death in order to appease the gods of nature.

To be honest, the place is nothing, when placed beside Machu Picchu, Tikal in Guatemala or the pyramids of Egypt. But it was fascinating to surmise about the lifestyle of these people and the fact they devised a sophisticated sewer system pre-dating civilizations considered raw and primitive. What did these people know that others didn't?

Even more interesting, was stopping in the villages where people you only see in National Geographic lived and survived on the land. But what land! Fields plowed on high, steep mountainsides, cultivated and harvested in all conditions of weather. Their homes are very rude adobe or thatched and when you look inside, it is dark, cavernous and very basic. In some, the blaring society of color TV's. The women wore lovely felt fedoras, more attractive than in Ecuador, with usually a feather design above the brim.

Where we were, higher up in the Cordillera Blanca, it was over 4,000 meters. On the way there, we stopped to drink tea steeped in cocoa leaves, which helped to considerably alleviate the ill effects of "altura" or altitude sickness. Returning to Huaraz, I felt ill and had to take one of the trusty pills I had bought in Quito. Gil, of course, suffered no ill effects, dang that man.

We plan to rest a few days here in Huaraz and then head back to Lima, which is about 380 kilometers, heading due southwest.

Our hostel, La Cabina, has a lovely view of the mountains, which surround the city and for 35 Soles ($11.50) per night for two, we have a large room and breakfast included. Our guide,Toushay, whom we met when we got off the bus, has been like a mother hen arranging tours, bringing me anise tea for an upset stomach and even tried to find a place where Gil could compress our digital photos. (No luck.) What a dear lady. We are always lucky to meet such wonderful, helpful people while traveling and she is certainly no exception.

Love from the Andean Travelers

ANDEAN VILLAGE NEAR CHAVIN

ANDEAN BOY WITH BABY ALPACA

HUARAZ

LIFE AS A NEW HOUSE

When my first husband and I had lived in our very first home for a few years, many of our friends started to move up in the world. The west end of our city began to stretch and expand like an old pair of maternity pants. Houses, the likes of which I had only viewed in magazines and on T.V., were being built thirteen to the dozen. Oak stairways curved into high-ceilinged bedrooms with crown molding and spacious walk-in closets. I toured four or five-piece ensuite bathrooms, complete with a small stairway leading up to a sunken tub with brass fixtures and, with the touch of a button, rippled waters Jacuzzi-style poured out. I oohed and aahed, slunk home and pined in private.

I tried to cajole my husband to consider a move, any move, but he was not one for change. Alas, I had married a man cast in wet cement. His employment at an auto parts factory and the purchase of our first home accelerated the hardening process. By the time I truly began to flex my female muscles, he was already hip-deep in solid concrete.

The idea of a new home, change, was daunting and expensive, too much for his Dutch-born frugality. I went out alone with a real estate agent to view possibilities but my husband's lack of interest cast a negative spray, which severely dampened my fledgling enthusiasm.

My yearning for a dream home was probably a mimicry of my yearning for a dream life. Whatever house you buy, however, a bona fide inspector could locate telltale faults in a heartbeat. The best 'fix' for a desire for change is children.

They came. They grew. The thought of moving – up, out, anywhere – was lost in a haze of diapers, bottles, trainers and parent/teacher meetings. Nurseries morphed into bedrooms for two growing boys. The basement was utilized as a teen's private cave. Parenthood suited me but somehow the crack in the marital foundation extended outward. So much so that the world began to notice.

A strange, debilitating illness reawakened my yearning soul and destroyed the façade. It was a curse, and a blessing, both. Scary and exciting, both. I lost my maternal girth and pursued spiritual, intellectual and artistic outlets. Meanwhile, my husband stood in the dust of my roadrunner's pace and scratched his confused, unchanging head.

A new home cannot answer your heart's yearning. Crown molding, Jacuzzi jets, formal dining room and en-suite bedrooms, fulfil but a heartbeat of desire. Perhaps my husband was right and I was wrong. Perhaps he was wrong; and I was right for the wrong reasons.

Kahlil Gibran once said that our homes were our 'larger selves'. What did he mean by that? Being a philosopher, he must have meant that a house is a soul and we must be careful and aware of what we decide to place within.

I yearned for inner fulfillment, but yes, I loved the idea of fires burning in a marble-mantled grate, overstuffed sofas and beds with a million pillows that take a half hour to remove at bedtime. I yearned for a room filled with bookcases I could fill with precious books, a writing desk and a window overlooking a pond where swans glide like clouds on a sunny day. Perhaps I was born in the wrong century or my soul hearkened back to a past life of contentment and gracious repose.

When I answered the siren call of a life on the West Coast of Canada, it was because I had met Gil. He became my 'new home' desire. I moved in and I proceeded to move the furniture around, toss out what did not suit and would have liked to gut the place and start all over again. You see what I am talking about?

My two men could not be more disparate in character. My first husband, Pete, feared change, stuck to the familiar, while Gil moved from home to home looking for – what? Before we got together, he revealed he had moved houses about 16 times, that home is wherever he happened to be. I guess I don't see it that way but also don't see it Pete's way, either. There has to be a happy medium. Fear of change and restless change are the symptoms of the same thing: Non-acceptance of who we really are.

It is all about acceptance, then. Acceptance of self, first and foremost. Everywhere, there are mirrors that reflect back to us our beliefs, eccentricities and shortcomings of character. The need to change others helps blind us to our need to change ourselves.

People come into our 'homes' for a reason. Perhaps they are remnants of our past not reconciled. Perhaps negative aspects that need polishing or removing. Perhaps a new challenge never before encountered.

I have met many people considered 'bad' but it was my bad choice that brought me too closely in contact with them. These were people who were 'Tricksters'. They led me or I allowed myself to be led, to believe they were what they were not. A façade of beauty, but once inside the door, a gothic horror. They were the best learning experience of all. Why? Because I learned to rely upon my 'gut' to inform me of the whereabouts of these lying souls and also learned to navigate through their hall of mirrors. They, especially, were not comfortable in their shoddily-built homes.

So yes, home is where our heart – and soul - is. You can decorate it any way you like but truly, it is the foundation that counts the most.

KILLING OUR CHANCES

With skill and daring
I will fight the weary lines
Etched
    painfully
    upon your face
But my anger, my fears
Are woefully
    displaced

It isn't time,
Cruel time
Drawing back its arrow
Time is blameless
Turn around
    And face
Who truly is our foe
Drawing back
    We take aim
Arrows of reproach
Sent dizzying high
Then
    finding their
        mark
Killing our chances

MIRAFLORES
(Lima, Peru)

After a few days, we said good-bye to Huaraz. We both suffered a case of traveller's flu and my altitude sickness grew quite debilitating. Gil wanted to take a bus to Barranca, halfway to Lima so we went to the station to purchase tickets. It was a double-decker bus and we sat right up top in front. However, the driver, a stingy sort, ran the air conditioning only occasionally and the sweat poured down our foreheads.

On the approach to Barranca, we realized we had made a mistake. The town was dusty, dirty and seemed a little frightening. Somehow, someone, must have been looking over us because the bus sailed right on by. We breathed a deep sigh of relief.

The bus then stopped at a compound where one could eat and take a bathroom break. The lineup to the woman's bathroom was about a mile long. There was a barrel of water and a cutout bleach bottle to flush the filthy toilets and, of course, no toilet paper. Some of the women got fed up and sailed into the *baño de caballeros*, but the chickenshit ones, like me, stood and waited.

Meanwhile, Gil went to the counter to buy a pop but the server deliberately ignored him. Time and again he tried but the man refused to serve him. A young girl took pity on him, placed his order on his behalf and he thankfully paid her. He was too frustrated to even attempt to order some lunch and we didn't know how long we had before the bus left. Later, we stood at a table near where the same young girl was sitting. She kindly passed over a banana to stave off our hunger. Then a nun came along and gave us a peach. For every jerk in the world, there are always two or more good people to make up for them.

Before we boarded the bus again, the same guy who'd refused to serve Gil was selling ice cream pops. Gil and I discussed the idea of tripping him so he'd lose his complete inventory but that would have been playing into the hands of those who are unable to set an example of kindness. The thought served to dispel the feeling of frustration and loss of control, just as one might imagine a roomful of people sitting naked, while giving a speech. However, thinking of this guy sans clothes, probably would have caused me to lose the little lunch I had eaten.

The road to Lima is lined with sandy cliffs dipping towards the ocean on the right and on the left, shanties planted on the sandy hills, huddling forlornly against the sky. We passed women washing clothes in an open sewer, even bathing their naked children in the filthy water and I felt too distressed to even take a photo. The busses congested the route into the city proper and it seemed to take forever to arrive at the terminal.

Since we considered our lack of air-conditioning and the abasing experience at the compound a fair trade for the free ride from Barranca to Lima, we said nothing to the driver, grabbed our luggage and hightailed it into the terminal. We tried phoning the *Hostal de las Artes* where we had stayed when we arrived in South America but it was full. A taxi driver suggested the suburb, Miraflores, and when we got there, we were glad he did. He found us a nice hostel on a quiet street and we began to explore this more upscale, touristy place.

We spent several hours visiting the huge Larcomar Mall, perched on the cliffs. It was very modern and the prices reflected its trendiness. The neighborhood was reminiscent of Vancouver's West End with its high rise apartment buildings, hotels and restaurants. We ate at a food court, watched the tourists and locals, then strolled through the broad expanse of streets filled with trendy boutiques, night clubs, coffee shops and ubiquitous Internet places. It was like cleansing one's palate of the unappetizing tin shanties, the dirt-poor, the tired looking hostels, the filthy bathrooms and endless beggars and street hawkers. It was a rich breath of fresh air.

On one of our many walks, we discovered a beautiful park down by the ocean (no bathroom nearby, though) and learned it was called *Parque del Amor*. An artistically landscaped garden and mosaic-tiled benches nudged up against the cliffs of Chorrillos overlooking the Pacific Ocean. Featured was a large, red sandstone statue of a couple, lying wrapped in each other's arms. I wondered how something like that would have been received in our neck of the woods. Probably protests, letters to the editor about how such a perverse piece of art might blight the innocent minds of children. Better to erect monuments to heroes of war, instead. We thought it a beautiful monument to love but what do we know?

Gil came down with what we considered a bacterial infection. No matter how many pills he took from the *farmacia*, he couldn't shake it. We assumed it was from the orange juice served at our hostel, but couldn't be sure. All we knew was he was unable to travel by bus to Cuzco. We had planned to visit Holly, our friend from Baños, at an orphanage in Huancayo, high up in the mountains and also go on to Nazca, famous for the etchings on the mountainside that can only be viewed from a plane. Perhaps on the way back.

We walked a lot in Miraflores and this served to dispel the tension between Gil and me. Usually our chosen destination dictated my moods and this section of Lima possessed a more European feel with its broad brick walkways edged with trendy shops and restaurants. We ate often at a particular Chinese restaurant and they got used to our faces, approaching us immediately with the local menu, rather than the higher-priced tourist menu. I felt content, not just for the idea of being in a place with a safe, continental flair, but with the knowledge that soon we will be going to Machu Picchu. Like a diamond glowing in the dark, it lulled and lured me at the same time.

I booked plane tickets to Cuzco and we were off the following day.

PARQUE DEL AMOR

LARCOMAR MALL

Miraflores

LIFE AS CHANGE

The anxiety of moving to the Island and renovating our very large house, stressed my relationship with Gil. That, plus the specter of our past habits and relationships.

These impersonal demons perched like vultures up on the rafters of love's home and waited for bodies to drop from arrows of blame.

Gil drinks, always has. Several cans of beer a night. I thought I had grown inured to the sound of the snap of the beer tab and the predictable ssshhhh as the brew released its pressure. Released his pressure.

As our problems mounted, I never noticed the Japanese maple outside my office window turn from a black-cranberry to a burnt orange. We had tucked our heads down for so long, spent so little time paying attention to the changing seasons and more time working, working on the house in Nanaimo, we'd lost touch. Especially with each other.

We are the culmination of our damaged relationships. There are always two who hurt, who withdraw and take longer and longer to come out of the cave to try again. Yet it is an ingrained need to always be on top, by pushing someone to the ground.

I wanted to stay home and write, but writing does not pay the bills. To see your words in print is a dream, he says.

Only one in ten thousand will get recognition. Like winning a lottery. I will win someday.

I once threw out at Gil, "If I had the money, I'd be gone!" Did I mean that? No, I still want to fight to be each other's greatest ally, fight for the right to stay by each other's side. I feel a shift inside me.

Autumn is a good time for change – new needs and wants issue forth. I want for myself now, not for others. I used to think if I loved and gave hard enough, there would be a payoff. But that gamble seldom pays off and the house always wins.

So isn't it better to give to the one who counts the most? I think so, too.

SERENITY

Fear has no place
Within
                    My serenity
If you had told me
I could
                    Feel this peace
I'd laugh in your face
Now laugh in mine

Give it time,   I know
Give it time,   they say
A new passerby+
Granted ingress to my place
My private domain
Move in
                    Change the décor
Move it this way to his taste
But not mine

Because I love you
                    Serenity goes
Out with the old
In with the new
My peace
                    Contentment
Tossed on the heap
Chased by fears of losing
You laugh in my face
Now I cry in mine

LIFE AS A TWO-CAR GARAGE

So many questions after my dad died. Questions like: Why did he enjoy visiting his gravestone before he died? Why did he set fire to our family home, a place that represented an almost-happy home to his family? Why did he have the power to invoke such misery into our lives, when he could have just as easily invoked a little caring, a little kindness or compassion? That last question is universal because we have all suffered under the yoke of someone else's negative power. As we grow older, the power structure changes yet we are still trapped in the dynamic of our past. We suffer from the mystery

Here's another mystery. It's called 'The Mystery of the Two-Car Garage'.

After my father effectively destroyed our family home down by the beach, we stayed with relatives while my parents searched out somewhere suitable to live. We went to view the house. I was about seven years old at the time. 'Suitable' was a small house on a street ending in a ravine. I went to the back yard and discovered a white trellis arbor with honeysuckle branches twined through it. I sat inside and felt wrapped in a sense of safety and peace. When we moved into that house, my father dismembered the little arbor, chopped down the honeysuckle vines and that was the end of my haven of peace.

My father decided to build a two-car garage. We already had a garage sufficient for our one and only car. In the small house we occupied, there were only two bedrooms for my parents and two eldest sisters. My brother slept on a couch in the living room and my sister, next in age to me, and I, slept on a foldout couch in the sunroom. At night my father kept the light turned on brightly while he rolled cigarettes on a newspaper and watched 'Hockey Night in Canada' on the T.V. Very loudly, because he was deaf in one ear.

Didn't my mother try to talk him out of this ridiculous undertaking? Why not build an addition onto the house to provide a bedroom for my brother and another for my sister and me? So there'd be no more groggy school mornings after late hockey nights and smoke filling our young lungs. My mother, through her silence and fear, gave tacit approval of my father's irrational determination to create an irrational reality.

Years later, I drove down that miserable street of my childhood. Someone had transformed that little house into a roomy backsplit. The bile rose up in my throat as the reminder of my father's selfish shrine rushed full bore into my memory. The reminder, that two-car garage he had built, had fallen into disrepair and was as badly in need of a coat of paint. It looked as old and weathered as the original had been, before my father demolished it to make way for this one.

One day, my sister encountered an old family friend on the golf course. This woman had been married to a very close friend of my dad's. She told of how her ex-husband and my father would get together and drink themselves into a stupor. Her ex was an alcoholic, which was why she divorced him and assumed my mother had divorced my father for the very same reason. We did not know our dad was a heavy drinker, let alone an alcoholic. We saw him merely as a man who changed his moods like flashes of lightning. When he struck, disappear.

On questioning our mother, she replied with an innocent, detached fragment of memory. Back when my father was constructing his two-car garage, he built a workshop complete with counter and large drawers below. My mother said, "Your father tried to entice me into the garage to share a drink or two with him. Inside the drawers was his private stash of gin, rye and whiskey. I always refused. You know I'm not much of a drinker..." She never thought he had a drinking problem, just a problem of personality.

What we thought was a shrine to his selfishness, was really a shrine to his weakness. Can I forgive him knowing this? That those erratic moods and irrational decisions, which caused his family such anguish and discom-

fort, arose from a weak character? Erecting a monument to protect his dirty, little secret?

He is dead and so, of course, I forgive him anything. But if he were alive would I go to him, try to dredge up the past, dredge up the truth, condemn him and then forgive and forget? We all look for reasons to explain the mysteries of our life and though the mystery was explained about the motivation of an irrational man, so many others remain.

Like me. What about the mystery of me?

WEARY WORLD

Where is this world
Taking me?
My steps so heavy
I follow and falter
I am not strong
It's not the world
Wearing my soul down
But my lack
I lost my hope
Down the road
And faith, I dropped it
Many miles back
I need a little luck
To retrieve it
But belief wore a hole
In my pocket
And God, where's God
Oh He fell through
The sidewalk cracks

THE DUKE AND THE COURTESAN

She taught me all the tricks of attracting a man. I was born in a small village in France, in the eighteenth century. My mother often took me to Paris, showing me off, waiting to sell me to the highest bidder. Her youth had lost its full blush but she was still beautiful and through me, she held on.

Because I was beautiful and intelligent, these two commanding qualities won me many rich and well-placed admirers. But mother waited until the timing was just right, then she found him: The Duke of Ormondy.

He was old, looked very old to me yet, he had a sort of panache about him and was an erudite and well-read man. I was not attracted to him in the sense of the physical 'him' but to the qualities of nature that defined the physical. The way he walked, how he held his head, his hands and how he made you feel as if you were the only person in the room. My mother chose well.

I was to be his lover. I did not object to this state of affairs but wanted to stay in the game, so did not relegate myself only to him. Over time, the lovemaking fell away and our evenings were spent talking books and ideas. He had a rapier wit and I matched him bon mot for bon mot. I think he fancied himself in love with me but I was young, so young, and there was still so much to see and do, so many places to visit, so many conquests to make; he did not understand.

I was away in Paris when I heard the news. Somewhere during my rounds, I received word that he had taken a wife. Not much later I learned that it was my mother who'd become the Duchess of Ormondy. I was shocked, yes, but then I felt a deep sense of betrayal, for I realized I loved this man and knew he still loved me. I made the obligatory trip to visit them, conferred upon the happy couple my congratulations. My mother had won and she knew it. My lovers dropped off after that. My conquests, my desire to savor life, tasted like ashes in my mouth.

I had enough money to retire so I returned home to the country with my companion, a lovely woman, who saw to my needs but sat as my equal. I visited the Duke and his lovely wife as seldom as I could, because when we saw each other, emotions too naked to trust shone in our eyes. Why, why did he marry her? Why could he not have waited until I was older and shed of my youthful exuberance?

We wrote each other, the Duke and I, usually every other day. My heart raced with joy when I saw his crescent seal on the salver when I came down for my morning repast. I knew he had married my mother to punish me and my mother realized the effects, but it was too late. She was his, and he was hers, to the end of their days. Their religion forbade it any other way.

He died, he simply died. I kept his letters and read them every day. Though my mother sought solace from her own daughter, I could never look to her for mine. She was not his match, never was and never could be. I refused to allow regrets to rule my life.

When I was ready to pass on, I knew he was there waiting patiently for me. How dapper and young he looked! He took my arm in his and we walked down the sun-drenched lane, apple blossoms floating on the spring air. The world and eternity must have thought us a well-matched pair.

This was another life with Gil. I even 'Googled' the 'Duke or Ormondy' and there was such a person who lived during the 18th century in France, although he was the Duke of 'Ormond'. Jonathon Swift made an oblique reference to him in his writing, as well. My logical, five-sensed self regarded it as a very large coincidence.

CUZCO and MACHU PICCHU

We had never visited a place that could wear one down so much as Cuzco. The street hawkers, shoeshine boys, indio craft sellers and people commissioned to pull you into a particular restaurant, never left us alone. Sometimes they followed us for blocks until we just wanted to run to our room and hide under the blankets. On one occasion, while walking down the main street, Gil said, "I'm going to count how many times we're approached." Over the next 3 minutes by his watch, once every 6 seconds.

As soon as we got off the plane, the native people waited to offer up cocoa leaves – for a price. You can chew them or steep them in a tea. The high altitude (3325 meters) found a lot of *turistas* being confined to their beds the first day. I still had my 'magic' pills from Quito so I was well ahead of the game.

The condor is a mystical bird in Incan mythology but I later learned it is a form of vulture, a predatory bird. This aptly described the atmosphere and behaviour of the tourist industry in Cuzco. No doubt, it is beautiful with its narrow, cobble-stepped streets and massive Incan walls. One young boy began to describe, in good English, the various blocks within these walls that represented serpents and animals, like the jaguar. We listened, hoping to learn more but he stopped in mid-tale and said, “I take Visa.” Can you take a hike?

Gil still suffered from his infection and we constantly needed to keep close to washrooms. We had booked into one hostel and found it not to our taste, so spent the better part of a day searching out another. Finally, we found a large one with three beds (for the suitcases, of course…), a bathroom plus breakfast. We found the manager/owner a bit dour at first but later learned he had a wicked, subtle sense of humor. Once, when I went out alone, I came back looking for Gil, who had ventured out while I was away. The manager suggested he was probably out chasing women, and I had to look closely at him to observe he was ‘pulling my leg’. After that, we never went in or out the front door without sharing a witty Latin barb or two.

I booked a tour to Machu Picchu. I knew Gil had never been interested and because of his uncomfortable ailment felt going solo would be a better experience. I paid $210. U.S. then realized later that the tour operator was barely legit. I didn’t sleep at all the night before, fearing to miss the pickup at 5:30 a.m. A woman and man arrived in a dilapidated mini-taxi and when we got to the train station, the train was just minutes away from leaving. The woman shoved tickets and itinerary at me. I ran through the gate and hopped the required train car, just making it by inches.

My seatmate was a former El Salvadorian named Anna Elizabeth. I was born Elizabeth Ann and thought this an interesting coincidence. We also had the same tour guide. Better and better. The journey was 3 ½ hours long (Machu Picchu is 70 km northwest of Cuzco), but flew by because we enjoyed each other's company so much. Anna lives in Toronto, just an hour away from my birthplace and works for World Vision. She was in South America to check up on various projects and needed a day off, so here she was and I was so glad.

The train arrived at Agua Calientes and there were busses waiting to ferry us up the steep, winding mountain that leads to Machu Picchu. Because I was so jaded from Cuzco, I reserved my great expectations.

At the top, we were encouraged to take a snack break and of course that was a ploy to get you to buy, buy. After a cola and some taco chips, the various tour guides appeared to herd their lambs. Ours was named Fabrizio.

Fabrizio truly was an ardent proponent of Incan ruins. While we walked through and climbed the majestic ruins with the green and gracious mountains in the background, the wild Urubamba River shooting rapids far, far below, he talked about the condor and what it represented to the Incan civilization. (I know what it represented to me!) The Incans were lovers of nature and the condor is the representation of the unity of the sky, earth and the underworld. All humans aspire to be one with the gods and it is through nature this can be realized. The condor hunts from the skies and when it espies creatures – some from the earth and some below – it swoops down, grasps its prey in its talons and then sweeps up to the heavens with its reward. It also represents reincarnation, a tenet of the Incans, where everything cycles and repeats, over and over again.

Fabrizio wanted to make it clear that the return of the condor was not to be compared with the predicted return of Jesus, but a spiritual rebirth. So much of the civilization of Machu Picchu is merely theory – how they lived, how they died and the way they appeased the gods with animal and virgin human sacrifices, in order to keep the cycle of life turning. Yet, they disappeared without a trace. How's that for a magical, mystery tour?

Anna and I stayed behind to thank Fabrizio for sharing his heart. He had talked so passionately and was gratified we paid tribute to something he felt so strongly about.

A light drizzle accompanied most of the tour. Anna and I walked about after our group disbanded, took digital photos of the alpacas grazing high above, the great valley below and any other vistas we might have missed during the tour. I tried to take in the mystical energy, tried not to allow such ostentatious displays of rampant tourism mar my experience. (The hotel adjacent to the ruins milked the gringos for $600. U.S. a night and its restaurant served a buffet for $30. a person. This is not to mention the t-shirts, mugs, you-name-it, near the site and down in the tarp-covered market in the village below.) Anna and I ate at a very reasonable restaurant down in Agua Calientes.

On the trek back down the mountain, young native boys dressed in Incan outfits of red with braiding and feathers on their heads, began to chase the bus. One particular boy magically appeared at every turn down the hill shouting and waving. We thought the bus driver rather callous for not stopping for the poor kid. The bus travelled at a good pace and yet there he'd be, ahead of us. We thought he must have taken up flying like Peter Pan, because no one could move that fast on foot. At the bottom, the door opened and there was the boy sporting a big grin on his face. He spoke a few phrases in several languages, a form of prayer and thank-you, then passed around his small, alpaca purse. Yes, another tourist ploy, but worth a few Soles for his tenacity.

Unfortunately, Anna and I were assigned different coaches for the ride back to Cuzco. I sat with a man from Uruguay and learned a bit about his country. But he had a bad case of smoker's breath, which prevented me from engaging him in too much conversation. The train personnel put on a fashion show and hawked their expensive wares the last third of the journey. Luckily, I met an American nurse who suggested a medication for Gil that might be very effective.

Many of the various tour operators met their clients in vans at a particular stop at a village, in order to avoid the hour-long switchbacks on the approach to Cuzco. It was tedious going but the night view of the city was breathtaking. Not surprisingly, my tour-operator was not there to pick me up in the dilapidated Austin mini, so I grabbed a cab to take me back to the hostel. Anna and I hugged, exchanged email addresses and I was on my way. The driver wanted to take me to a disco, but I declined. What a gracious guy!

What message can I bring to you from Machu Picchu? The fact of meeting Anna represented a sense of common ground. That we are all one – under the sun, on the ground and even below, where our bones join with the earth. Politics, religion or skin colour should not separate us because we are all looking for the same thing: a little magic in the form of caring, compassion and peace. The big question is not where this particular civilization disappeared to, but where is our civilization headed? Will we disappear without a trace and will the theorists swoop down, write books and documentaries while the money-grubbers take advantage of the mystery, by creating myths of our disappearance in order to sell expensive tours and t-shirts?

We'd had enough of Cuzco and tried to change our flight but our air miles company said there were no flights and would not reimburse our travel miles. (You probably know who they are!) We had been told, when we booked our trip, there would be 'no problem' but this was not the case. Even when I solicited their compassion about Gil's medical condition, they were not moved. However, if we wanted to book a new trip, use new air miles, well, we could leave tomorrow. (These people should sell tours in Cuzco.)

We went to a travel agent and booked a flight to Mexico City. I cannot say I am sad to leave South America, though it has been an interesting ride and will provide fodder for many tales to tell the grandkids.

As for Machu Picchu, that remains to be seen, or felt. I like to think that some mysterious energy, perhaps extraterrestrial, penetrated my being while I innocently wandered those eerily empty ruins. When life gets a little rough, perhaps they will locate my whereabouts back home on the Island and beam me up. When the time is right. Maybe they'll have me head up a Star Fleet Federation.

Hey, it's my dream.

LIZ, THE GREAT EXPLORER OF MACHU PICCHU

MACHU PICCHU

COKE BOTTLE BABY - CUZCO

CUZCO

MEXICO CITY

Email to Family and Friends
February 16/07
Dear All: We are tired and jet lagged in Mexico City. We booked a flight from Cuzco and when we got to the airport, there was a mix-up as the travel agent put both of our flights in Gil's name. Because we were forced to wait to have this corrected, they upgraded us to Executive Class, all the way. We flew back to Lima, stayed overnight, then flew to Quito the next day, then to Guayakil, then to San Jose', Costa Rica and on to Mexico City. Our luggage flew direct. However, it didn't get to use the VIP lounge and be served fancy meals in roomy, comfy seats on the plane like we did.

Our connections were very close and we arrived in Mexico City at about ten in the evening. The airport is 'ginormous' and we were even exhausted from riding the many people movers. Gil had booked us a hostel near the University. First we had to pre-pay our transportation at a kiosk, based upon distance and then be escorted to our taxi.

The hostel was very misleading compared to the Internet ad and a real comedown from Executive Class. We had a room with no bath, bunk beds and were given sheets to make our own beds. The bathrooms were very dicey. I had to get up early in the morning to answer nature's call. I trundled down the hall and when I went to sit down, noticed just in time the toilet had no seat. Plus, someone had left a 'gift' in the bowl. By this time I was wide awake. I went to the other bathroom and this one had no door handle but I had closed it without thinking. Getting ready to scream for Gil, I noticed part of the door handle on the floor and used that to jimmy my way out. In the morning we got the hell out of there.

We decided to stay at a 'real' hotel at the north end of the city near the bus terminal, since we planned to go to San Miguel de Allende in a few days.

We took a bus and walked around the Central District of the City. It smelled like a cesspool. If the smell had a sound it would be a deafening roar. Their sewer system, I assume, is not very efficient, which has taken away my enjoyment of the ancient churches. Many had stood for centuries withstanding earthquakes and all manner of historical upheavals but I wonder, can they withstand the reek?

While we strolled the streets, riot police were everywhere. Not to keep the 'turistas' in order but to keep a watchful eye on the people who protested the government's expropriation of their residences. When we queried a citizen, he told us that these places were drug houses and the new government was cracking down on them. We took a lot of photos and in case you are wondering, we were not picked up, put in a paddy wagon, but are still here, we didn't disappear. So far.

People here in Mexico City are not as friendly as the people in South America. The busses pass you by if you are not fast enough and many of the people play dumb if you ask for directions or try to communicate with them. It is a big city but so was Quito and we experienced mainly goodwill, kindness and helpfulness there. Here, they want your tourist dollars but get the hell out of my face. In Ecuador and Peru, our families worried about us, but here...well, they should worry about us here.

Gil has already figured out the subway system, got his trusty map and is rarin' to get going. To get from one end of the city to another will cost a whopping 25 cents (population is 30 million in this city, can you believe it?). I am jetlagged and feeling a bit sick. He can conquer the City on his own peso. While he plans to visit the Anthropological Museum, I am going to call for room service and spend the day in bed. We plan to book a trip to San Miguel de Allende in a few days.

Love from the world-weary travelers.

DIEGO RIVERA MURAL, NATIONAL PALACE

CATHEDRAL - MEXICO CITY

PALACIO DE BELLAS ARTES

METRO, MEXICO CITY

LIFE AS A FIELD OF DREAMS

Our days inside that little house on the street that ended in a ravine, were seldom happy. My father had a way of turning everyone's light into darkness. So we kids spent most of our waking moments out of doors. We came inside to eat or go to bed. We played baseball, played in the ravine, in our tree house or in the field behind our property. The grass in that field grew very high, a great place to play hide-and-seek. For me, it was a place to build my very own house.

Walking around, I'd stomp down the high grasses, usually into neat squares. Between each square I'd flatten narrow passageways. It wasn't a large house, but for me it was just right – four or five rooms. I added a few closets and a bathroom. However, I didn't want reality to intrude upon my little dwelling. Reality was my father and my unhappy life in our real, little house just a property away.

I'd go into my completed home and lie down in my living room, grab a long stalk of grass, suck it between my teeth and gaze contentedly over what I had created. Closing my eyes and feeling the sun soak over me, I'd picture myself in my future. My happy future, in a real house. This one made of glass or brick, maybe cedar. Instead of tall grass, there'd be an ocean outside my window and maybe some mountains. Filled with happiness, no darkness allowed.

When I grew up, I married a man who was never unkind to me but our feelings never joined. I thought the pain I felt was of my own creation. I thought perhaps I could tamp it down, thus create a fantasy in the midst of my reality. Not too large and it would hold a future of light and acceptance. Yes, ever the hopeful little girl, lying in my sundrenched field of dreams, sucking grass and waiting for a happy future. It should have been mine. At least by now.

MY MEDIEVAL DREAMS

O what alchemy I could
Mix up in my magic chamber
Hidden deep within
Too long a doormat, too long a dust
Collector, memo minder
List maker, orange squeezer
O the medieval magic I could spin...

Castles on fairy mounds, dragons flying
Flapping bronze-veined wings on the wind
Wimpled ladies, visored knights and steeds
Restless on the cobbled bridge as his master
Plumes a poem of love and his brave deeds

But then real life tears me back
When I hear the shuffle of the postman
Sliding my mail through a slot
The mortgage on the castle need renewing
The cobbles need repaving and the steed's
In need of reshoeing and the old visor's shot
The dragon chewed his way through the fence
I need a new ink cartridge for the plume
My wimple could use a good dry-cleaning
There's the lease for the fairy mound
Prices have soared out of sight
Like my medieval dreams, I've found

MI COMPLEAÑOS IN MEXICO CITY

February 18th was my birthday. We left the hotel and went for breakfast. The waiter, an older Mexican, ignored me completely. It was obvious he didn't like women or perhaps North American women. I tried to communicate with him but he pretended not to hear or understand me. He deferred to Gil, shook his head in my direction, looked to him to translate my idiocy. I felt as if I didn't count or exist. After we ordered, or Gil ordered, I began to cry and Gil asked me why.

"It's my birthday. I'm still so far from home. I miss my family so much and a Mexican waiter is treating me like crap. Is that about it in a nutshell?"

I had wanted some toast, bread and jam, but instead I got two halves of a large bun, all greased from the grill with what I assumed was melted cheese on top. It was unpalatable and most likely indigestible so I left it untouched. The waiter served Gil his fried eggs, frijoles and tamales with a flourish and I wanted to punch out his lights. Gil shared his breakfast with me while Nazi Waiter looked on with disgust. Happy Birthday to me.

Dixie, our Lady of Wisconsin, had suggested we visit the Basilica of the Guadaloupe Virgin Mary, located ten minutes north of our hotel. It was reported that several miracles had happened there and a shrine had been built around them. The original shrine had sunk into the earth, so they erected a new one adjacent to it. (If I prayed hard enough, I might have my own little miracle, like turning that misogynist waiter into a five-inch female midget so I could dip him, like a lady finger, into my breakfast coffee.)

The taxi driver over-charged us (80 pesos or 8 US dollars) for a five to seven minute ride. He dropped us off at a market area where there were tents and each one hawked the same things: gaudy pictures and trinkets of the Holy Virgin. Gil had an idea to buy a clock to place it above these people because it was Sunday and time for church, not time to be marketing religion, but practicing it. Talk about your golden calves…

We walked around the park surrounding the shrine. The grass was green and shorn like a golf course. There were fountains adjacent to the new and old churches. People, alone or with family and friends, waited for the mass to begin. Some bore massive bouquets to offer up at the altar. Many got down on their knees, walked on their knees towards the church.

Children were placed upon fake ponies to have their pictures taken with a myriad of Virgin pictures behind them. A cameraman was at the ready to digitalize the scene forever. Getting ready to ride into the sunset with the ultimate heroine.

Everything was immaculate, the reason being, signs that could have been written by the Virgin herself, exhorting the populace to keep 'her' garden neat and clean. Considering the state of Mexico City – garbage on the streets, the beggars and the hungry, roaming dogs and human gangs – it was obvious this was the only place the plea would have been answered. Outside the shrine, everyone for himself.

Later, we took a bus downtown to the *Palacio de Bellas Artes* to see beautiful murals by Diego Rivera, Mexico's premier artist. A mural commissioned by Rockefeller but later destroyed, was re-created here by Diego. Why was it destroyed? Because it deified socialism and vilified capitalism, all that Rockefeller epitomized. Rivera had perversely painted the face of Lenin in the mural. He and Frida were avowed communists but the rich American who commissioned his art was not. We loved the fact Rivera represented the common man and also that he illustrated him in control of his destiny and his technology. The name of the mural was, "Man at the Crossroads."

We eavesdropped on a tour and learned a lot about Rivera and how he included Frida Kahlo, the famous Mexican artist and his wife, in his art. In one painting we saw, at the National Palace, he had painted her holding a severed arm. She had had a near-death experience and was plagued by images of death. Many of Rivera's murals illustrated cruel images of slavery in Mexico's early days, while money-lenders are depicted with greenish, ghoulish faces. You could spend a whole day looking at just one painting and feel you can never see and learn enough.

We took the Metro to a suburb called Coyoacan to visit *'La Casa Azul'* or the Blue House, which housed many of Frida Kahlo's personal effects and artwork. It took us about an hour to get there, got lost in the maze of streets. When we arrived, we learned the place was closed for renovations and no amount of whining and cajoling would cause the workers to allow us in for a sneak peek.

We took a side trip to San Miguel de Allende the next day. It was truly Americanized and the house prices reflected this. We met Julie, an American ex-patriot, who worked pro bono at the daycare for working Mexican mothers. She rushed to assure us she didn't associate with the 'gringos'. I guess they have a bad 'rep' here. It was said Americans adopted Mexicans when they arrived, like they adopted pets, then abandoned them when they left. I don't know how true this is, but sitting in the zocalo visiting the shops, I observed what I thought were a lot of pretentious gringo types.

At a book store, a tall, grey-haired gent walked in, wearing black corduroy pantalons and black lederhosen.

I walked in the town square beside a white guy trying to emulate Lawrence of Arabia, with his long, flowing headdress and safari outfit. We could see the line of demarcation here and we believed this was because the locals probably worked as their maids and gardeners. I don't know – if I had to choose between a guy in lederhosen and a hard-working, unpretentious Mexican, it'd be a no-brainer.

Gil and I ate in the local market, where the food was cheap and delicious. We were usually the only white folks there, but were always treated well, although still considered a kind of oddity.

On the bus to San Miguel, we met two teachers from the Bronx, Patricia and Mary. Gil and I spent most of our time with Pat while Mary went off on various tours by taxi. Pat is tall, very thin and this from the stress of being a special-ed teacher of troubled teens in one of the roughest areas of New York. We spent one evening drinking Margaritas in the lovely town square, talking about life. She wanted to solve my problems with Gil, but the main issue is we've been in each other's faces for almost four months, so who wouldn't have issues?

I loved Pat's accent. Just like one of the characters of 'Saturday Night Live', Linda Richman, but that character was Jewish and Pat is Irish-American. 'Wanna go for cawfee? Let's tawk. Get outta heah!"

At an Internet café, we booked our trip home. This meant returning to Mexico City and staying another week. Gil was anxious to get back on the Metro and conquer the rest of that big, polluted and rude city. Oh yeah, right behind ya, hon…

In general, I much preferred Peru and Ecuador. The people were kinder, more engaging and less 'Americanized', more independent. Here they're dependent upon the almighty American buck, though I'm sure they hadn't noticed they've morphed into greedy facsimiles of what they claim to despise.

With the exception of the rampant commercialism of Cuzco and also Machu Picchu, many places in South America were lovely and untouched, their innocence still intact. For me, it was being so far from home that was the scary part, not the people. I was not afraid to walk around Mexico City by myself, however, because the *policia* are everywhere in evidence, the crime cleaned up considerably. But in South America it was the pride of the people I admired, while here in Mexico City it is nowhere in evidence.

Gil and I took the Metro. We saw very few tourists taking this mode of transportation, save for young backpackers or the odd, curious traveller, like us. Some of the Mexicans engaged us in conversation and asked where we were from, and some stopped to help us when we were not sure which route to take to get to the zoo.

One day, Gil went to check out the price of electronics and I wandered the streets by myself. Somehow, I got lost and decided to ask a newstand proprietor for directions to our hotel. He began to yell at me in Spanish, and then waved me rudely away. As I walked away, I threw back at him, "A***ole!" He understood my English perfectly because his voice grew louder and I could hear him offloading his vitriol halfway down the block. I was so pissed off, I found our hotel.

As for my relationship with Gil, it suffered even more. He took up drinking again because, as he said, it didn't make any difference in our relationship. Whether he drank or not, we still couldn't get along. In our hotel in Mexico City, I told him, "Gil, I don't like you anymore. This trip has been difficult but even more difficult with your controlling ways. So many times, I've felt as if I was your secretary or a witness on the stand. I'm tired of it. Let's continue the journey as acquaintances and see what happens." And so we did.

I needed to feel in control because I was afraid I had lost control of myself.

LIFE AS TRUTH

It wasn't long after my grandfather died, that my grandmother remarried. Being an outgoing and vivacious woman, I'm sure she had her pick of all the available men in town. The one she picked proved to be a very affectionate stepfather. As a matter of fact, as my mother and her two sisters grew older, he became even more affectionate. Sometimes, it was not enough to keep him from cuddling them too much at bedtime or even later on, when all the lights were out in their little house in that rural Ukrainian community in Saskatchewan. I guess that's another thing my mother never forgave her mother for.

To be honest, I don't think her mother really cared about what her daughters thought. If her husband was a little tardy coming to bed, or if she awoke and found he was not beside her, she most likely turned over and went back to sleep.

My mother had a cow she raised from birth. This animal was her baby, her pet and she lavished upon it all the love displaced from her father's death. A natural affection, but the affection her stepfather lavished upon her and her sisters alarmed and frightened her. Finally she told her mother. Whether her mother believed her daughter about her husband, or not, didn't really matter. What mattered was that a woman in those days needed a man to run a farm, to take charge of the family and represent a good standing in the community. A daughter's complaint was a threat to that standing.

The solution to the problem was simple: sell the cow to buy a railroad ticket to send my mother to relatives in Ontario. Sell the cow my mother loved, petted and fretted over from the day it emerged from its maternal womb. Another dreadful loss in her life.

A sixteen-year old arriving in the big city from an ignorant country town, is prey to all manner of wolves. These wolves survive by projecting their illusions upon poor, unsuspecting sheep, by masquerading as sheep themselves. My mother was ripe when my father entered her life. Twelve years her senior, he was handsome, well dressed and eager to rescue and protect her from harm. Like a wolf protecting the hen house.

Did my mother need to be rescued from the pain she suffered as a child? Did she need to be rescued from her innocence, for her own good? Did she need to be rescued from herself so she didn't have to take responsibility for her life that was and her life yet to be? Here, sign on the dotted line. Now I have you, my pretty.

There is a moment in time in my mother's life with my father that encapsulates their life together.

It was the middle of the night in our little house ending on a ravine. My mother awoke bleeding profusely, then she began to hemorrhage. My father slept on. My mother was too afraid to disturb him, so she phoned the ambulance and waited at the door, losing a great deal more blood from her body. The ambulance attendants looked for someone who should have been looking after this woman, protecting her and keeping her warm and safe. My father was warm and safe, snoring in his warm, selfish bed. Still sleeping, while my mother almost bled to death.

I remember little of that night because everything was muffled, the memory like a distant voice in sleep. But later the truth supplied, in early adulthood, by my elder sisters. I felt such pity for my poor mother, such anger for my cruel father. I wanted to enact retrograde revenge on her part, but his life was his retribution. (He died alone; no one came to check up on him. His landlord found his body after he had been dead three days.)

I look at myself and my sisters and wonder about our own choices. Perhaps we were not victims in our relationships but enablers, giving power to our rescuers and those we have rescued. Did our genes inherit this ability, was it thrust upon us through our father's abasing abuse or was it unfinished business from a past incarnation?

My complaint from my English lifetime as a lonely, rich girl was, "I had no support in my life. No one supported me - emotionally." I was rich, but very poor. Then I came back into this life yearning for the very things I yearned for in that life. My mother was the epitome of yearnings unfulfilled.

When my father greedily, cruelly, burned down our house at the beach, he tore from me my idyll, just as my mother was torn from her life by the avarice and callousness of another. For her part, she gave up and lapsed into medicated mental illness and who could blame her? Sometimes I wanted to give up, too.

In my first marriage, I sold my soul for my sense of security but life happened and the growth of my spirit forced me to make changes, which involved meeting Gil and moving thousands of miles away to be with him. Yet, our life together has been one challenge after another. Where two, strong swords cross, there is bound to be sparks.

If I say that my mother signed her life away, would that be callous? If I say that she gave power to those who victimized her, would that be cruel? Has my enlightenment of self, precluded compassion? Yes, of course, I do feel compassion for my mother and her very hard life, but it is a detached compassion. I felt I needed to distance myself from her as a way of learning the lessons she didn't. When other people or family members say I resemble her physically or in certain emotional reactions, I say to myself, "Oh, no." I wanted to erase her from me because I fear our biology might become my destiny.

But, what a groundless fear. Every experience molds us by our reactions to them, making my mother and me so different from each other. Every choice we make or do not make, forges us into who and what we are. The past leaves us or we leave our past yet, it is forgiveness, which clears the way to our better selves.

More than anything, we must forgive the wolves, especially the ones who hide behind covers of a benign façade. Then we must forgive ourselves for believing in them in lieu of believing in ourselves. Then we must learn to speak our truth. Not in a forceful way, but with a gentle, strong voice. The ears that need to hear it will listen, and the ears that cannot or will not, are not meant to hear it. Maybe, at a later time.

> **Truth may not be forceful - it relies for its efficacy on a willing and free acceptance, but it can heal. It can even repair a broken world. Like sanity, truth is grounded in the soil of the real world, as we ourselves can be thought of as being derived from the soil of the real world. Truth poses no threat to anyone save those who rely on untruth as the cornerstone of their foundations. It is time to speak the truth- irrespective of who is listening or even has the ears to hear.**
>
> **~Anonymous**

Email to Family and Friends
March 3/07

Dear All: We are now safely home on the Island. I was never so glad to leave a place in all my life. Time and time again, the inhabitants of Mexico City treated us like dirt. Many times in restaurants we had to practically beg to be served, then we were served last. But when it came to the bill, they were right there with their hand out.

We can assume they thought we were Americans. But I would not assume that any dark-skinned person coming to my country was from, for example, Africa, and since I had an issue with that country, treat that person with disdain. In Peru and Ecuador, they always asked, "De dondé vas?" Where do you come from? And we told them. They wanted to know all about us and we filled them in. We told them we wanted to learn their language, so please correct us and many took the time to do so. In Mexico, they waved us away or ignored our attempts. We felt safe, but unwelcome. Some have likened these people to the Parisians, who are arrogant and intolerant.

But now, we are home, jet lagged and out of sync, but will adjust soon. We flew from Mexico City to Los Angeles, then had to change airlines, which meant rushing to get our luggage. Our plane arrived an hour late and our luggage didn't make it to Vancouver. My eldest sister, Sally, from White Rock and my son, Rob, were there to meet us at the airport. Our luggage was delivered the next day to my sister's condo and thankfully was not checked. We had bought a plethora of pirated movies, so were relieved not to have had them confiscated. My sister delivered us to the ferry this morning and our good friends, Ron and Sue, picked us up on the other side. We took them to lunch, bought a few groceries and they dropped us off here at our trailer, No. 409 at Surfside R.V. Resort. How heavenly.

Thank you for joining us on our journey, supporting us and

generally 'gentling' me along when I got tired, fed up and didn't want to continue. Knowing you were out there made it much more valuable to me, as the trip did not feel as strange or scary. (Well, maybe not all the time...)

We are going to sleep for three days. Don't wake us up until next week.

Love from the Landed Andean Travelers

HOME SWEET HOME

PUTTING IT ALL TOGETHER

Reviewing my past lives, I felt the need to encapsulate the experiences in one neat, package. I asked my son, who led me gently through most of these incarnations, what he felt were common factors or patterns.

"Looking at your lifetimes, I saw extremes. The life as a nun, as opposed to a courtesan. The life as a 'pagan' healer, as opposed to the nun. The life as the spoiled, rich girl, as opposed to the devoted, Cathar husband and father. Extremes of experience that gave texture to your life and the life of your soul."

For me, it was the pattern of my mate, Gil. In my lifetimes as the rich girl, the aboriginal and the nun, the love I shared with him was never out in the open for the world to see. We were forced to go underground because our society did not approve. Whether it was differing stations in life, the taboo of religion, differences of age or tribe or the dynamics of inner motion, we could not share our hearts and souls openly.

Gil's lifetimes were a matter of extremes, as well. He was a charming odd-job man, as opposed to the priest. The rich duke, as opposed to the poor lover of the rich girl.

Positions of power and positions of powerlessness. In all, he possessed the same charm and charisma he possesses today.

Sylvia Browne once said that planet Earth is a 'boot camp' for the soul and truer words were never spoken. It is hard, heartbreaking, soul-searing and humanely callous. Man's inhumanity is an ongoing vicious cycle. If we are proponents of the concept of reincarnation, then we take turns in roles of victims and victimizers. My lifetime as a Cathar showed me as both because I sought revenge for the death of my family by betraying my religious community. I felt guilty because I could not protect my family and therefore blamed my group because they were powerless to protect the soul group from annihilation. It was a twisted form of "do unto others…" My twisted psyche evened up the score by causing the burning death of my community and then taking my own life.

The idea of compassion is the common thread through any and all lifetimes. But it is compassion to the self, first, that must be accomplished before we turn and offer caring to others. If our hearts are empty, then that is all we can offer to the world.

At the end of my session with the hypnotherapist, a revelation struck me about another pattern of this lifetime and others. I opened my eyes and said, "I had no support!"

The troubled rich girl had no one to lean on, no one to pat her on the back and let her know she was 'okay'.

To me, the pattern continued into this lifetime because my family was fragmented by the paradigm of a father who ruled with an iron fist and a damaged heart.

The stigma of my skin condition set me apart from my family and society. If I drew up the contract before my incarnation as 'me' then I also created an extra burden of a being whose feelings of unworthiness were written all over her body, for the world to see. And we all know how cruel people can be. Even my own family could be cruel by saying things like, "The reason you don't have any friends is because of your skin!" No, the reason I didn't have any friends is because I felt unworthy.

Once, I was in an upscale restaurant with my mate. In walked this beautiful girl with long, black hair and a lovely face. She was wearing a revealing outfit and she was covered in psoriasis! All I could think was, "Wow!" The courage it took for her to 'reveal' herself put me to shame. But it also gave me the courage to slowly reveal myself, and my lack of perfection, to the world.

We all have our burdens and imperfections. We look to others for support and acceptance but often what we need does not materialize. Usually, we receive it when we least need or expect it.

I walked away from my family years ago for several years because, instead of supporting me during my separation and divorce, my sisters supported my ex-husband because they viewed my joining with Gil on the West Coast of Canada as a form of desertion – of them and my sons. I heard many recriminations through the family grapevine, causing me to suffer inwardly and outwardly with the stigma of guilt, causing many skin eruptions. I could not make up to my sons enough, could not spend enough on them when they came to visit. Could not support my eldest son enough when he moved close by, though it impacted my relationship with Gil and my relationship with self.

I suffered breakouts from feelings of rejection and guilt. But, then one day, I made up my mind, “Enough is enough.” I decided to ‘give over’ and give myself a break. No, I could not look to others to give me the approval and validation I needed; it had to come from elsewhere – from within.

We read a lot of hokey psychology and spirituality about nurturing our ‘inner child’, but it is so true! Author Wayne Dyer suggested, in one of his books, that the reason there are so many people with mental illness is because of one’s family. So many poor souls left dangling, waiting for even one, just one, kind word that will set them free.

One day, the phone rang and it was my estranged sister from back East, who was next in age to me. Her daughter was getting married and could I come to the celebration?

This was the first time we had talked in nine years. We talked for what I thought was a long time and then when I got off the phone, I shared with Gil. Should I go or shouldn't I?

"You have to go. You know you have to, just to prove you can."

"I know but first there is the issue of money. I'm not in the position to pay for the air fare, the rental car, other expenses."

"First, you can use my Air Miles. Then go from there."

As it turned out, the money materialized, seemingly out of thin air. I received a cheque for editing work and then, out of the blue, another cheque arrived from the government that exactly covered my rental car expenses. The doors opened.

I had a great time at the wedding and also spent time with my youngest son, Mark. I renewed my strained relationship with my eldest sister, who lives on the mainland and from that reunion, we continue to enjoy each other when I take the ferry there or she comes here to the Island.

Each of my sisters has said to me at different times, "You are the sister I really connect with." And I know why: Because it no longer matters what they think of me

I learned to detach myself from the dynamics of others. A great counselor said to me, " Others' opinion of you is none of your business."

Revisiting my lifetimes has slowly released me from my pain of unworthiness, my pain of caring too much what others think and feel about me. I've learned to detach and focus on what is important to ME, not what is important to everyone else.

The journey to South America was very important to Gil, but not important to me. To help fulfill his dream, I went along 'for the ride'. I resented the experiences and blessed them at the same time. Because, that outer journey to two strange countries helped me look at life in a new and different way.

Learning about other countries and cultures is like exploring other lifetimes. From all these experiences, perceptions morph into realizations. So many realizations. I perceived myself as an open-minded person, but then realized I was so open-minded some of my brains fell out. One can get pretty self-righteous at times, yet my inner and outer journeys have virtually wiped the smirk from my smug face. Humbling, but empowering, at the same time.

You fly to the moon with an idea in your head. On the moon, it's the 'wow' and the oohh and the aahh, then the flight back home. Tired and rocket-lagged, it takes time for the body to adjust, for the mind to process. Then the heart and soul takes over.

Let it.

A SHORT AFTERWARD

Gil and I still occupy separate trailers at Surfside. But this has turned out to be the best thing that has ever happened to us. We are both learning to let go and let each other be.

I've learned that in my accusations of his controlling behaviors, I have been guilty of the same thing. Our counselor called it 'mirroring'.

We are learning to be each other's best friend. When we get together we laugh, share, support each other and yes, we make love, but it is a freeing experience rather than an obligatory one. There is no doubt we love each other. After so many lifetimes of constraints and our controlling habits in this one, the idea of creating a new dynamic is exciting. You have to 'join' before you can join.

As for my skin, onward and upward. I found a wonderful naturopath and he placed me on a regimen to cleanse my liver, restore natural flora to my intestines and remove any trace of candida in my system. By staying away from milk products with milk fat and opting for yeast and wheat-free products, I can trace the physical patterns. What I put in my body is entirely up to me.

What I put in my mind, heart and soul is up to me, as well.

FINIS

GUIDED MEDITATION FOR PAST-LIFE REGRESSION

(Ensure the subject is comfortable, whether on a chair with high back or supine on a couch or bed. It is important that he/she be warm, so provide a blanket or throw, and pillows are better flat than full. Background music or a tape of the ocean or a mountain stream set low, lends to a soothing backdrop. Turn off the phone, pull down the blinds and it is nice to have a lit candle to augment the spiritual mood. You are ready to begin.)

Just feel your body relax, breathe deeply and easily. Know you are surrounded by the white light of the Holy Spirit. Release any negative energies from the past and during the day. Allow them to flow out of your body, down through the soles of your feet and be released down deep into the waiting earth. Let your conscious mind recede and any thoughts, let them fall away. Allow your unconscious mind to come forward as they are the seat of your memories.

Starting with your feet, feel each muscle, bone and tendon of your toes relax. Feel the soles of your feet give way and melt, melt. Allow your ankles and shins to ease any tension you are holding, and then release, relax. Feel the warmth pulsate into your shins then into your calves. Feel each muscle, bone and tendon as if they were butter and placed in the sun's rays. Allow your knees to melt, relax and give way. Relax your thighs and feel the warmth travel and pulsate up into your waist and on into your lower back. Deep in your solar plexus, feel the deep, warm relaxation. Imagine all the organs inside your body surrounded and flowing with golden, liquid light. Surround your spleen, liver, kidneys, stomach and heart with soothing, warm liquid light. Feel that light travel to your upper back and diaphragm, into your chest, easing and pulsating with relaxing warmth.

Breathe deeply and with each breath, feel yourself melting away. Relax your neck and shoulders, allow them to slightly tense and then relax, relax. Feel the warmth travel down your arms, forearms and down into your hands. Tense, release and relax. Relax your lower jaw, allow it to go slack and let your tongue fall to the floor of your mouth.

Feel the muscles and bones of your face relax and give way – your cheeks, nose, forehead and even your ears. Feel the warmth pulsate into the back of your neck and on into your skull then feel the top of your head opening to receive any spiritual assistance. Any angels you feel close to, like Michael or Raphael, call them to stand by and protect you during this regression.

Now, breathing deeply, I want to ask you whether the

issues you are dealing with concern this life or a past life. I will count to three and you will tell me. One, two, three...

(If a present life) *Now let's go back, back to a time in this life when your issues or problems began. Okay, how old are you now? Where are you? What are you doing?*

Lead slowly and carefully, allowing for pauses etc. If there is a moment of agitation or an upsetting incident, suggest emotional distance, as if viewing on a movie screen. It is important that forgiveness is shared with those the subject feels has wronged them. Also that a contract was made between them and that forgiveness must be asked of the other to make the pact complete. If need be, 're-script' certain moments. If a certain action was not done or needed to be done for healing, or something not said needed to be said in order to empower the subject, then suggest they do so.

(If a past life) *Imagine walking on a forested path. Feel the pine needles scrunching beneath your feet and notice the sunlight dappling through the trees. Feel the warmth of the sun rippling down your shoulders and how peaceful you feel. In the distance you can see a small cottage. It has a rustic porch, shutters and roses growing on an arbor in* *front. Walk towards it and enter the wooden door, then step into a lovely parlor. There is a chair in front of a crackling fire and in the next room a small library filled with shelves of books, from top to bottom. One of those books has your name on it. Take it down and place it on the oak table in front of you. Inside is a map of the world and taking a pencil or pointer, raise it above your head. Quickly bring it down upon a certain country in the world. When I count to three, you will tell me. One, two, three...Okay, where are you? Are you a male or female? What are you wearing? What are you doing?*

Again, do the forgiveness prayer. When departing from that life, ask what needed to be learned and was the lesson complete? Ask who was waiting for them when they shed their bodies. Sometimes subjects have gone to the Hall of Records to look in the book that reveals their life path to see if they are following it.

If there are other lifetimes that need reviewing, ask if the subject wishes to continue to explore. If yes, then give a reminder about breathing deeply and relaxing and continue to explore other lives.

(When it is time to return, reverse the relaxation.)

Now slowly move your arms and legs, slowly awaken each

part of your body. Remember what has taken place to take into your day. Open your eyes and tell me if you are truly in the 'now'.

Give a glass of water or brew a cup of tea and review, if needed.

My son and I practiced with each other several times. We completely trusted each other so had no difficulty getting under. He is visual and could see and describe everything in perfect detail. I was more 'feeling' and learned to rely upon my intuition to guide me.

Release expectations of what you perceive exploring previous lifetimes is about. Contrary to popular thought, you are always in control at every moment, viewing and selecting or rejecting what is significant for you.

This is not a parlor game. Ensure your intentions are true and sacred. Protect yourself and your aura with the white light of the Holy Spirit.

Many of my subjects, who were non-believers in past lives, were often the easiest to put 'under' as there were no expectations of outcomes. Expectation is a conscious way of thought, so it is important to ease it back and allow the unconscious mind to reveal and bring out what is most needed for psychic healing.

Disclaimer

The Guided Meditations for Past-Life Regression
are not intended nor claim to fix anyone's problems.
It is best to explore with the professional guidance of
a certified hypnotherapist or certified life coach counsellor.

ACKNOWLEDGEMENTS

Sue Ouimet at Little Mountain Publishing, helped me get this book off the ground, by spending so many long hours with me, polishing the text and walking me through the technical jargon of the publishing process. I couldn't have done this without you. Also a big hug to her husband, Ron, who patiently allowed me to 'borrow' his wife when he would have liked her all to himself.

Thanks to Gil Roy, my special partner, who tolerated my homesickness on our Andean trek and encouraged me to keep going when all I wanted to do was sit down on the side of the road and give up. Also for reading and re-reading my manuscript, making suggestions and providing missing elements, facts and perceptions that I had somehow forgotten on our journey.

To my son, Robert J. Julian, who pulled out of me much more feeling than I was initially willing to divulge. Sometimes I felt I was a dry well but you took your dousing wand and tapped a new one, releasing a wellspring of thoughts, memories and sometimes very painful emotions. Yet it gave a new dimension to this book and I will be forever grateful for that.

A big 'thank you' to the women of Pen & Inklings writers' critique group of Delta, B.C. (Dolores, Kim, Alice,

Laura and Rae), who helped me learn how to edit out the 'junk' and find my voice. Your kindness, support and expertise gave me the confidence I needed to keep going, keep writing and, well - keep writing.

Thanks to founders of the Nanaimo Metaphysical Network (NMN), Myrtle, Christina and Judith and William Munns. who were my spiritual mainstays. Before that, it was my meditation group in St. Catharines, Ontario. Especially Cliff and Linda Preston, whose guidance helped me find the way to a new life on the West Coast.

Finally to my dear friend, Janie (Lockhart) Nicholls, who cared enough to read my stories and help me believe the world will also want to read them. Your ongoing friendship got me through some tough times but it is your wacky humour that always took me over the top, from high school to now. Still Ginger to your Fred on the garbage cans.

A Short Bio

Liz Roy was born and raised in St. Catharines, Ontario. She now lives on Vancouver Island with her soul partner, Gil Roy.

Made in the USA